Moorman Family Ancestors

Ellsworth and Eva Moorman Family

Compiled and edited by Joni Wilson

ISBN: 978-1-7333158-5-2

Gracious Lily Publishing

Cover photo: Eva and Ellsworth Moorman and five of their six children, Knob Noster, Missouri, circa 1930s. Left to right: Florence, Harry, Ella, Erwin, Oscar, Eva, Ellsworth. William Oral, their fourth child, died age 1.

Disclaimer

Most of the information contained in this book was acquired through online sources, primarily Ancestry, which was made available at no charge to Mid-Continent Public Library (Missouri) users.

While every effort has been made to verify the information, there are limitations. Not all records are currently available online. At the time of this writing, US Census records were only available through 1950. Not all states and countries allow free access to birth, death, marriage, divorce, or burial records.

Volunteers may enter data incorrectly, especially when attempting to spell names that have been poorly handwritten in the original sources. When the online sources give other spellings of names, those variant spellings are given in this book.

If readers have information that is different from what is provided, please contact the editor and corrections will be made in future editions.

Note: Most of the first-generation individuals are deceased. However, a few are still alive as of this writing. In those cases, minimal information is given to protect their privacy. In some places, the first generation's children, grandchildren, and great-grandchildren names are given, but no further information is given.

Genealogy

You are about to enter a world that is partly an art, partly a science, and mostly frustration! While you think you are looking for information about the lives and relationships of your ancestors, you are really not prepared for what you may find.

You think you know who your family is (was). Remember, they are humans who lie, cheat, steal, kill, commit adultery, and all sorts of other unsavory things. Then you'll get to the bad folks in your tree! You'll find that other "genealogists" haven't been quite as diligent as they should have been. (Oops, we left lazy out of the above list of sins!)

So how should you tell the story of your lineage? Should you be "prudish," thinking my relatives could never have done that! Oh, yes, they could . . . and did! Should you be "kind" and decide that [someone] doesn't need to know who her father really was?

We need to remember that genealogy is what it is . . . a study and documentation of the lives of people; the good, the bad, and the ugly. Don't we owe it to ourselves and future generations to report it in as accurate a way as possible by telling like it is (was) while remaining sensitive to the feelings of the current generation?

—Paul Andre, Columbia, Missouri

Contents

Introduction

While researching the life of Virginia Merle Moorman, information was discovered about many of her ancestors. This book details the family line of Oscar Myron Moorman, Virginia's father. Another book will provide information about the family line of Gela Lela Cook Moorman, Virginia's mother. Using online websites and Virginia's notes, names, birth and death dates, burial locations, spouses, and children were located. While some of these are simply names and dates, it is interesting to see where the Moorman maternal and paternal families originated and how far they traveled to live in various places.

Where known, the cause of death and the age when the person died has been listed. From the 1500s to about 1800, people in Europe lived between 30 and 40 years of age. In the US, life expectancy in the 1860s was about 40 and rose to about 80 in 2020. It dropped during the Civil War (1861–1865), World War 1 (1914–1918), and the Spanish flu epidemic (1918–1920).

It was also interesting to see the number of children (where identified) and how many were born in a seemingly short span of time. On the **Moorman maternal** side, the average number of children that families had was 6, ranging from 4 children to 9 children in the family. The children were born over an average of 17 years, ranging from 7 years to 23 years, and there were three sets of twins. Ancestors were born in Connecticut, Massachusetts, Michigan, New York, Pennsylvania, Rhode Island, and Scotland.

On the **Moorman paternal** side, the average number of children that families had was 7, ranging from 1 child to 19 children in the family. The children were born over an average of 16 years, ranging from 1 year to 37 years. Ancestors were born in Delaware, England, Ireland, Kentucky, Maryland, Michigan, Missouri, Netherlands, New Jersey, North Carolina, Ohio, Pennsylvania, Scotland, and Virginia.

The **Moorman maternal** family life expectancy (for adults listed in this book) was 66 years old for females and 51 for males, ranging from 26 to 99 years old at the time of death. Cause of death included cirrhosis, arteriosclerosis, pneumonia, lung cancer, tuberculosis, old age, senile dementia, sudden heart failure, fever, tuberculosis, exposure, cancer, accidents (one from poison gas from a well and one from falling rock in a coal mine). There were six recorded deaths of children from 1 day to 8 years old (measles).

Several men from the **Moorman maternal** family served in the military, including the American Revolution, the War of 1812, the Civil War, and World War 2. Five brothers from one family served in the Civil War on the Union side; four survived the war and one died from a fever during the war. Another Moorman served in the Civil War and discharged with a disability. At least four men served in World War 2; two survived the war and two died. One was a flight engineer—his plane was shot down over France; he received a Purple Heart. One was a pilot whose plane likely experienced mechanical failure and he was lost at sea near England.

The **Moorman paternal** family life expectancy (for adults listed in this book) was 60 years old for females and 69 for males, ranging from 22 to 91 years old at the time of death. Cause of death included pneumonia, murder, suicide, fall backward, infirmities of old age, cystitis, coronary occlusion, arteriosclerosis, shock after operation, apoplexy, consumption, cerebral thrombosis, hypertension, emphysema, lung abscess, breast cancer, cirrhosis, and one was a patient at an asylum. There were 16 recorded deaths of children ranging from 5 months to 19 years old.

Several men from the **Moorman paternal family** served in the military, including the British Army, the American Revolution, the War of 1812, the Civil War, and World War 1. Nine members of one family served in the Civil War on the Union side. At least 17 Moorman men served, mostly from Iowa, but also in units from Ohio, Illinois, and Maryland. According to a Moorman family member "the family was divided, half for the North and half for the South." One brother was killed because he appeared in a Confederate uniform. One died from "disease" during the war, one was killed in battle, and two were discharged with disabilities.

In the 1800s, many Quakers (**Moorman paternal**) left Virginia to travel to Ohio because of slavery. Many thought they couldn't live in a community where slavery was an economic cornerstone. Others migrated because of the Revolutionary War. If a Quaker member joined the Army, he was disowned by the Quakers. After the war, they were often reinstated to the faith. These soldiers received land from the government for services rendered, and often the land was in Ohio.

The Meaning of the Moorman Name

The Moorman family is of English extraction. The name is derived from moor, the prairies or commons of England— "man of the moor." Long before the Revolution the Moormans, who were Quakers, left their country to avoid persecution, and emigrated to America.
—Sketches of the Moon and Barclay Families; including the Harris, Moorman, Johnson, Appling Families

The Moorman family is purely Saxon, of English extraction. The name is derived from the Moors—as the prairies of that country are called—that is Man of the Moors, or Moorman . . . The motto of the Coat Arms of the Moorman family is "Esse Quam Ridero," which, translated, means "To be, not seem to be." —Mrs. James E. O'Donnell

Color Coding for Maternal Moorman Ancestors

The following color coding has been used to help readers trace the generations.

First generation: parents, aunts, uncles
Second generation: grandparents, great-aunts, great-uncles
Third generation: great-grandparents
Fourth generation: great-great-grandparents
Fifth generation
Sixth generation

Virginia Moorman's father was Oscar Myron Moorman.

Oscar Myron Moorman's mother was Eva Estella Beebe Moorman.

Eva Estella Beebe Moorman's parents were Myron Francis (Sr.) and Ella Doolittle Beebe.

Myron Francis Beebe Sr.'s parents were Gideon Morgan and Adeliza "Eliza" Allen Beebe (Keeler).

Ella Doolittle Beebe's parents were John A. and Mary Jane Smith Doolittle.

G. Morgan Beebe's parents were **Samuel** and **Elizabeth "Eliza" Thomas Beebe**.

Eliza Allen Beebe's parents were **John S.** and **Permelia "Amelia" Pinckney Allen**.

John A. Doolittle's parents unknown.

Mary Jane Smith Doolittle's parents were **Ebenezer** and **Polly Clark Smith**.

Maternal Moorman Family

Summary of Maternal Sixth Generation and Beyond

Samuel Beebe traced to the 12th generation in 1570 with origins in Connecticut and England. A family member relates that he was a jeweler of "Scotch" descent.

Elizabeth "Eliza" Thomas Beebe. Unable to find any ancestors.

Samuel (24) and Eliza (19) married about 1803 (unknown location). They had 8 children in 13 years.

Gideon Morgan Beebe is the Moorman family ancestor. See details in the Maternal Fifth Generation.

~~~

John S. Allen traced to the 7th generation in 1803 with origins in Connecticut; traced to Michigan. A family member relates that he was English-Nova Scotia.

Permelia "Amelia" Pinckney Allen traced to the 10th generation in 1642 with origins in Connecticut, England, New York, and Rhode Island. A family member relates that she was "Dutch-Pennsylvania, German."

John (19) and Amelia (19) married about 1822 (unknown location). They had 9 children in 23 years.

Adeliza "Eliza" Allen Beebe is the Moorman family ancestor. See details in the Maternal Fifth Generation.

~~~

John A. Doolittle's parents unknown. John is the Moorman family ancestor. See details in the Maternal Fifth Generation.

~~~

Ebenezer Smith traced to the 10th generation in 1626 with origins in Connecticut, England, and Massachusetts. His father, Captain Oliver Smith, "fought in the Revolution" and was imprisoned by the English. He and six other soldiers escaped and nearly resorted to cannibalism before being rescued.

Polly Clark Smith. Unable to find any ancestors.

Ebenezer (26) and Polly (25) married about 1823 (unknown location). They had 7 children in 12 years.

Mary Jane Smith Doolittle is the Moorman family ancestor. See details in the Maternal Fifth Generation.

~~~

Moorman Maternal Ancestors

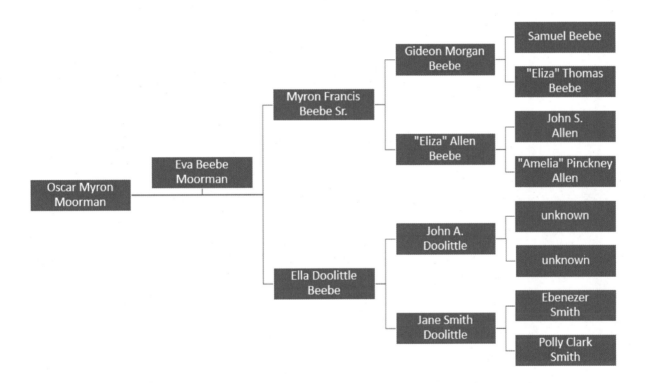

Moorman Maternal Family Ancestor Locations

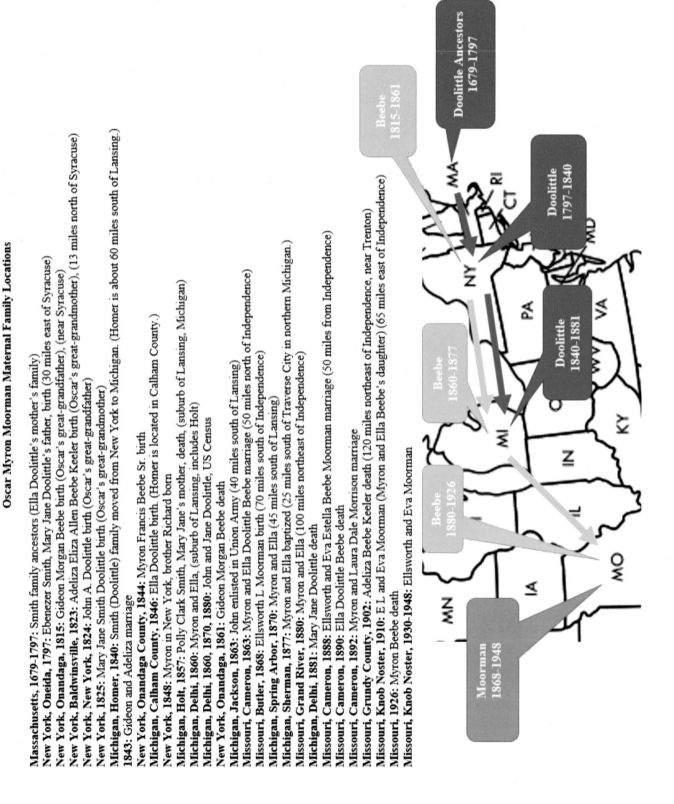

Oscar Myron Moorman Maternal Family Locations

Massachusetts, 1679-1797: Smith family ancestors (Ella Doolittle's mother's family)

New York, Oneida, 1797: Ebenezer Smith, Mary Jane Doolittle's father, birth (30 miles east of Syracuse)

New York, Onandaga, 1815: Gideon Morgan Beebe birth (Oscar's great-grandfather), (near Syracuse)

New York, Baldwinsville, 1823: Adeliza Eliza Allen Beebe Keeler birth (Oscar's great-grandmother), (13 miles north of Syracuse)

New York, New York, 1824: John A. Doolittle birth (Oscar's great-grandfather)

New York, 1825: Mary Jane Smith Doolittle birth (Oscar's great-grandmother)

Michigan, Homer, 1840: Smith (Doolittle) family moved from New York to Michigan. (Homer is about 60 miles south of Lansing.)

1843: Gideon and Adeliza marriage

New York, Onandaga County, 1844: Myron Francis Beebe Sr. birth

Michigan, Calham County, 1846: Ella Doolittle birth. (Homer is located in Calham County.)

New York, 1848: Myron in New York, brother Richard born

Michigan, Holt, 1857: Polly Clark Smith, Mary Jane's mother, death, (suburb of Lansing, Michigan)

Michigan, Delhi, 1860: Myron and Ella, (suburb of Lansing, includes Holt)

Michigan, Delhi, 1860, 1870, 1880: John and Jane Doolittle, US Census

New York, Onandaga, 1861: Gideon Morgan Beebe death

Michigan, Jackson, 1863: John enlisted in Union Army (40 miles south of Lansing)

Missouri, Cameron, 1863: Myron and Ella Doolittle Beebe marriage (50 miles north of Independence)

Missouri, Butler, 1868: Ellsworth L Moorman birth (70 miles south of Independence)

Michigan, Spring Arbor, 1870: Myron and Ella (45 miles south of Lansing)

Michigan, Sherman, 1877: Myron and Ella baptized (25 miles south of Traverse City in northern Michigan.)

Missouri, Grand River, 1880: Myron and Ella (100 miles northeast of Independence)

Michigan, Delhi, 1881: Mary Jane Doolittle death

Missouri, Cameron, 1888: Ellsworth and Eva Estella Beebe Moorman marriage (50 miles from Independence)

Missouri, Cameron, 1890: Ella Doolittle Beebe death

Missouri, Cameron, 1892: Myron and Laura Dale Morrison marriage

Missouri, Grundy County, 1902: Adeliza Beebe Keeler death (120 miles northeast of Independence, near Trenton)

Missouri, Knob Noster, 1910: E L and Eva Moorman (Myron and Ella Beebe's daughter) (65 miles east of Independence)

Missouri, 1926: Myron Beebe death

Missouri, Knob Noster, 1930-1948: Ellsworth and Eva Moorman

Samuel Beebe

Born 15 Feb 1779 (Saybrook, Connecticut); died 23 April 1819 at age 40 (Onondaga, New York). Probable burial location is Onondaga Valley Cemetery, Syracuse, New York. "Ancestral Chart"[1] lists Samuel as "Jeweler, Scotch descent" but his known ancestors were from England. He likely served (24 Oct 1814–15 Nov 1814) in the War of 1812 (also known as the Revolutionary War) as a sergeant under Commander Arnold Foote. Samuel married Elizabeth "Eliza" Thomas (1784-1819) about 1803. They had 8 children. When Samuel died, he had a last will and testament, dated 29 Mar 1819. He left everything to his wife, Elizabeth.

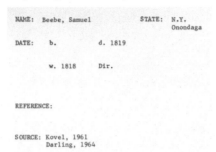

```
NAME:    Beebe, Samuel          STATE:  N.Y.
                                        Onondaga

DATE:    b.            d. 1819

         w. 1818      Dir.


REFERENCE:


SOURCE:  Kovel, 1961
         Darling, 1964
```

US Craftperson Files, 1600-1995, silversmith. Note: The "w" is for his work residence during this year.

~~~

Samuel Beebe's Ancestors beyond Sixth Generation

7. Samuel Beebe's parents were **Samuel Beebe** (15 Feb 1752, Saybrook, Connecticut; after 1794, Saybrook, Connecticut) and **Jerusha** (1753-?). Jerusha's parents unknown.

~~~

8. Samuel Beebe's parents were **Edward Beebe** (1709, Haddam, Connecticut; 20 May 1786, Essex, Connecticut) and **Hannah Pratt** (19 Jan 1718, Saybrook, Connecticut; 23 Jul 1790, Essex, Connecticut). Edward and Hannah married in 1737 (Saybrook, Connecticut) and had 5 children. Hannah's parents unknown.

~~~

9. Edward Beebe's parents were **Thomas Beebe** (1682, New London, Connecticut; 1740, New London, Connecticut) and **Anna Hobson** (4 Feb 1693, New London, Connecticut; 15 Nov 1725, New London, Connecticut). Thomas and Anna married in 1707 (New London, Connecticut and had 4 children. Anna's parents unknown.

~~~

10. Thomas Beebe's parents were **Samuel Beebe** (23 Jun 1633, Broughton, England; 12 Mar 1712, Plum Island, New York) and **Mary Agnes Keeney** (1640, New London, Connecticut; 9 May 1725, New London, Connecticut). Samuel and Mary married in 1660 (Connecticut). Mary's parents unknown.

~~~

11. Samuel Beebe's parents were **John Beebe** (1600, Broughton, England; 18 May 1650, onboard ship prior to arrival in America) and **Rebecca Ladd** (30 Oct 1602, Broughton, England; 1650, Broughton, England). John and Rebecca married in 1627 (England). Rebecca's parents unknown.

~~~

12. John Beebe's parents were **John Beebe** (1570, Great Addington, England; 30 Jul 1638, Broughton, England) and **Alice Stratton** (1580, Broughton, England; 1624, Broughton, England). John and Alice married in 1599 (England). John's and Alice's parents unknown.

~~~

---

[1] Nine pages in possession of the editor that were in Virginia Dungan's papers. These appear to be genealogy pages completed by Jennie Fern Beebe Lloyd, daughter of Myron Francis Beebe Sr. and Laura Dale Morrison Beebe.

Elizabeth "Eliza" Thomas Beebe

Born 23 Sep 1784; died 27 Aug 1819 (Onondaga, New York) at age 35 (three months after Samuel died). Probable burial location is Onondaga Valley Cemetery, Syracuse, New York. She had her first child at age 19 and her last child at age 31. Eliza died three months after Samuel died. Her children were ages 4 to 14. In her last will and testament, Eliza left everything for the maintenance and education of her children. Unable to trace the ancestors of Eliza Thomas Beebe.

~~~

Samuel and Eliza Beebe Summary

Samuel Beebe (24) and Elizabeth "Eliza" Thomas (19) married about 1803 (location unknown). They had 8 children, one set of twins (all born in Onondaga, New York), in 13 years.

1. Francis (8 Dec 1803; 1 Nov 1820, New York) died age 16.

2. Richard (11 Sep 1804; 2 Mar 1847, New York), farmer, married Iantha Webster (1805; 1879). Iantha died of consumption. They had 7 children: *Samuel Wyman* (1825; 1875) schoolteacher, *Charles Kasson* (1827; 1898), *Caroline Elizabeth* (1827; 1895), *Edwin L.* (1831; 1904), *Wallace W.* (1833; 1884) farmer, *Hannah Amanda* (1835; 1849), *George W.* (1839; 1912).

3. Samuel Arthur (22 Jun 1806; after 1860, New York), farmer, married Caroline E. Webster (1810; 1852). They had 6 children: *Ellen* (1828; 1850), *Edwin* (1832; 1850), *Elizabeth* (1837; 1850), *Frank Carter* (1844; 1920), *Arthur* (1848; 1916), *Kenneth* (~1852; ?). In the **1850 US Census,** brothers Richard and Samuel and families lived next to each other.

4. Eliza (19 May 1808; 21 Aug 1818, New York) died age 10.

5. Zalmon Lawrence (21 Oct 1810; 28 Apr 1868, New York), attorney, married (1) Catherine "Kate" S. Hopper (1816; 1855) in 1844. They had 5 children: *Charlotte E. "Lottie"* (1847; 1923), *Zalmon Lawrence* (1848; 1902), *Catherine H. "Kate"* (1850; 1914), *Z. Louise/Louisa* (1852; after 1925), *Mary Ella* (1855; 1881). After Kate died, Lawrence married (2) Harriett "Hattie" C. Thompson (1829; 1877) in 1857. They had 3 children: *Harriet J.* (1858; 1917), *Lillie Lucie* (1859; 1878), *Flora Susie* (1861; after 1875).

6. Lucy M., twin (21 Oct 1810; 1885, New York) married Christopher Columbus Conklin (1813; 1888). They had 4 children: *Samuel B.* (1844; 1912), *Oscar* (1848; 1914), *Adelbert D.* (1850; 1921), *Henry J.* (1853: 1934). Christopher died from "softening of the brain."

7. Susan/Susanna E. (29 Sep 1812; after 1870) married Joseph James Chase (1820; after 1870). They had 5 children: *Marian E.* (1843; after 1860), *John Wesley* (1845: after 1870), *Sophia S.* (1851; after 1870), *Ella J.* (1854; after 1870), *Bertha A.* (1859; after 1870).

8. Gideon Morgan (20 Aug 1815; 26 Jan 1861, New York) married Eliza Allen (1823; 1902). They had 4 children. See details in Maternal Fifth Generation.

~~~

Left and middle: Samuel and Eliza's son Richard Beebe, Onondaga Valley Cemetery, Syracuse, New York, died age 43. Right: Samuel and Eliza's son Z. Lawrence Beebe, Onondaga Valley Cemetery, Syracuse, New York, died age 57.

Samuel and Eliza's daughter Lucy Beebe Conklin, Onondaga Valley Cemetery, Syracuse, New York, died age 74.

~~~

Gideon Morgan Beebe is the Moorman family ancestor. See details in Maternal Fifth Generation.

~~~

John S. Allen

Born 1803 (Connecticut); died 1864 (Delhi, Michigan) of tuberculosis and exposure at age 61. John and Amelia Pickney (1803 or 1804; 1886) married about 1824 (New York).

According to "Ancestral Chart," he was English-Nova Scotia. He said he was descended from Ethan Allen. However, current research has not verified this. He had his first child at age 19 and his last child at age 42. The obituary for John B. Allen (son) said that he and his father (John S. Allen) moved to Michigan [between 1855 and 1860] before the Civil War, clearing the land and building a log home. When it was completed, John B.'s mother (Amelia) moved from New York to Michigan. The **1860 US Census** shows Amelia and the children living in Michigan, but there is no mention of John S. Allen.

If John had been diagnosed with tuberculosis, it was likely that he was in a sanitarium for treatment, although there were no specific treatments (other than rest, eat well, and exercise outdoors) nor were there special treatment facilities in the state of Michigan at that time. During the 19th century, tuberculosis was the leading cause of death in the US. It was characterized by fatigue, night sweats, a persistent cough, and general wasting.

> My father, Myron F. Beebe, said "The Allens were all fair complexioned, — all blonde, —no dark eyes. All were of stocky build, some short some tall, (men) but all heavy. No drunkards, non-religious, but sober and industrious. All Democrats. There were no paupers among them. They had no physical peculiarities. They were not a high-tempered people. My grandfather, John Allen, claimed to be a descendant of Ethan Allen, leader of the 'Green Mountain Boys' in the Revolutionary War. He was a very large and powerful man; and his son, William, was like him. He died of consumption (T.B.) caused by exposure. He was the only one of the family to die of this disease." —From "Ancestral Chart"

John S. Allen's Ancestors beyond Sixth Generation

7. John S. Allen's father might have been **Abraham Allen** (no details). John's mother unknown.

~~~

Permelia "Amelia" Pinckney Allen

Born 1803 or 1804 (New York); died 27 Dec 1886 (Alaiedon, Michigan) at age 83. John and Amelia married about 1824 (New York). Buried Markham Cemetery (Holt, Michigan). According to "Ancestral Chart," she was a Dutch-Pennsylvania, German lady. Amelia's father died when she was 7 or 8. She married about age 18, had her first child about age 19, and had her last child about age 41. After her spouse died, when she was about 60, she resided with several of her children in Michigan.

Permelia "Amelia" Allen, Markham Cemetery, Holt, Michigan, died age 83.

Permelia "Amelia" Pinckney Allen's Ancestors beyond Sixth Generation

7. Permelia "Amelia" Pinckney Allen's father was **Elijah Pinckney** (25 Sep 1771, Somers, New York; 1811 Onondaga, New York) and mother was **Margaret Polly Lyon** (~1781, Rhode Island; 1852, Onondaga, New York). Elijah and Margaret probably married about 1800.

~~~

8. Elijah Pinckney's father was **Gilbert Pinckney** (3 May 1743, Mount Vernon, New York; 6 Jan 1819, Somers, New York) and mother was **Mary Sebe "Sybil" Townsend** (~1747, Mount Vernon, New York; 30 Jun 1840, Urbana, New York). Gilbert and Mary married about 1765. Mary's parents unknown. Gilbert served as a private in the "War of Revolution" Third Westchester County Militia.

> 51. Gilbert Pinckney,⁴ son of Jonathan³ and Sarah (Ward) Pinckney, married Sibel Townsend. He removed from Eastchester to that part of Cortlandt's Manor now known as Somers, Westchester County, N. Y. He was a private in Third Westchester County Militia in War of Revolution. March 19, 1815, he conveyed to Lancaster Underhill his interest in lands in Eastchester of which his father, Jonathan Pinckney, died seized. March 13, 1805, he executed his will, which was proved January 11, 1819; in it he names his sons, Charles, Elijah, John, Jonathan, James and Gilbert and his daughters, Elizabeth, Alche and Anna, and his granddaughter, Rebecca. Children:
>
> 87. Charles,⁵ born May 29, 1766; died October 13, 1836, at Red Mills, N. Y.
>
> 88. Elizabeth,⁵ born September 11, 1767; died 1844; married Robert Lounsberry.
>
> 89. Alche,⁵ born September 22, 1769; married Caleb Marshall.
>
> 90. Elijah,⁵ born September 25, 1771; died 1811-12.
>
> 91. Ann,⁵ born January 11, 1775; died unmarried.
>
> 92. John,⁵ born July 17, 1777; died unmarried at Aurelius, N. Y.
>
> 93. Gilbert,⁵ born May 3, 1782; died August 11, 1837, at South Onondaga, N. Y.
>
> 94. Jonathan,⁵ born May 3, 1782.
>
> 95. James,⁵ born May 1, 1785; died November 26, 1853, at Aurelius, N. Y.

North American Family Histories, 1500-2000.

Margaret Polly Lyon's parents were **John Lyon Jr.** (3 Apr 1760, Foster, Rhode Island; 14 Mar 1814, Foster, Rhode Island) and **Phoebe Theodora Carpenter** (1764, Voluntown, Connecticut; 11 Apr 1814, Foster, Rhode Island). Phoebe's parents unknown.

~~~

9. Gilbert Pinckney's parents were **Jonathan Thomas Pinckney** (1687, Eastchester, New York; 1777, Mount Vernon, New York) and **Sarah Jane Ward** (1 Nov 1698, Westchester, New York; 1743, Eastchester, New York).

John Lyon Jr.'s parents were **John Lyon** (1740-1803) and **Martha Burlingame** (1744-1825). John's parents unknown.

~~~

10. Jonathan Pinckney's parents were **John Pinckney** (1642, England; 1725, New York) and **Hannah Hunt** (1655, Eastchester, New York; 1698, Eastchester, New York). John's and Hannah's parents unknown.

Sarah Ward's parents were **Edmund Ward** (1670, Fairfield, Connecticut; 27 Jun 1712, Eastchester, New York) and **Mary Hoyt** (22 Dec 1664, Fairfield, Connecticut; 1770, Eastchester, New York). Edmund's and Mary's parents unknown.

Martha Burlingame's parents were **Daniel Burlingame** (1718-1794) and **Martha** (11 Jun 1744, Rhode Island; 1825, Chenango County, New York). Daniel's and Martha's parents unknown.

~~~

John and Amelia Allen Summary

John S. Allen (19) and Permelia "Amelia" Pinckney (18) married about 1822 (location unknown). They had 9 children (all born in Baldwinsville, New York) in 23 years.

1. Gilbert (1822; 1862) died of fever in the Army during the Civil War, married Mahala.

2. Adeliza "Eliza" (Nov 1823; 1902, Michigan) married (1) Gideon Morgan Beebe (1815; 1861) in 1843. They had 4 children. After Morgan died in 1861, Eliza married (2) John Keeler (1837; 1905) in 1870. See details in Maternal Fifth Generation.

3. John B. (23 Dec 1825; 18 Dec 1925, Michigan) married (1) Anniebel Dunn (1829; after 1857). They had 1 child: *Ida May* (1857; 1901). John married (2) Jannette Hogle (1834; 1909). They had 2 children: *Parmellia "Millie"* (1874; 1962), *Eugene L.* (1876; 1963). John died of "senility" at age 99. Enlisted to serve in the Civil War, but a farming accident mangled his leg, and it was amputated.

4. Anne (Anna on death certificate) (13 Sep 1830; 13 Dec 1900, Michigan) married Norman Brooks (1827; 1909). They had 3 children: *Martha Amelia* (1848; 1921), *Harriett "Hattie"* (1850; 1860), *Burdette Ambrose* (1866; 1936). Anne died of "general debility" at age 70.

5. Martha (9 Aug 1833; 12 Jan 1901, Colorado) married Benjamin "Ben" Walter Holley (1832; 1911). They had 6 children: *Cecil S.* (1854; 1905), *Celia E.* (1855; 1876), *Merrill* (1859; 1871), *Ethel* (1863; 1952), *Arthur* (1867; 1868), *Shirley* (1872; 1974).

6. Elijah (4 Oct 1838; 15 Oct 1899, South Dakota) married Estella "Stella" Doolittle (1846; 1891). They had 4 children: *Charles I./D.* (1868; after 1880), *Ella C.* (1869; after 1880), *Carl/Earle E.* (1873; 1937), *Oliver G.* (1877; 1910). Elijah served on the Union side in the Civil War (1861–1864), was pensioned, died of old age. Lived next door to Myron and Ella Beebe in Michigan in 1870. Stella and Ella were twin sisters.

> 1st Sgt., Co E., 8th MICH Inf. Enlisted in on 23 Sep 1861, promoted to full sergeant on 15 Oct 1863. Attached to on 07 Jul 1863. Promoted to full 1st Sgt on 24 Jul 1864. Mustered out on 01 Mar 1864. Mustered out on 22 Sep 1864 at Near Petersburg, VA, record of service of MI volunteers 1861–65. He survived the war.

7. William H. (1839; 1880, Michigan) married Sarah "Sally" Grovenburgh (1845; 1928). They had 4 children: *William E.* (1863; 1900), *Carrie E.* (1864; 1879) died of scarlet fever age 13, *George E.* (1869; 1918), *Mabel Clare* (1880; 1959). William H. served in the Army during the Civil War—not well afterward, died instantly of heart failure "past middle age." After William H. died, Sarah married Albert A. "John" Holcomb (1833; 1925) in 1913 (Michigan).

8. Orisavila (1843; 1925, Michigan) married William N. Dunn (1840; 1929) in 1865. They had 4 children: ***Dana E.*** (1866; 1918), ***Della J.*** (1868; 1959), ***Edith M.*** (1871; 1966), ***unknown name*** (died in infancy). Orisavila died of "senile dementia" at age 82. William served in the US Civil was with Company B, 7th Michigan Volunteers. He was wounded in action in Virginia on 5 May 1864 and later promoted (to sergeant) for bravery on the battlefield.

9. George W. (1845; ~1922) married Emily Fletcher (1841; after 1900) in 1875 (Illinois). They had 1 child: ***Guy Fletcher*** (1877; 1951). In the **1900 US Census,** Emily (married) was living with her son Guy in Rock Island, Illinois. George is not listed as part of the household. George was a schoolteacher, served in the US Civil War, died age 77.

~~~

John and Amelia's son John B. Allen, Markham Cemetery, Holt, Michigan, died age 99.

John and Amelia's son John B. Allen (1825-1925) death certificate, died age 99.

LACKS BUT FIVE DAYS OF LIVING 100 YEARS
JOHN ALLEN DIES AT DELHI HOME FRIDAY.
Cleared Land For Log House Where He Passed Most Of Long Life.

Lacking only five days of having lived a full century, John Allen, passed away at the home of his daughter, Mrs. George Painter, in Delhi township on Friday evening, December 18. He had been slowly sinking for the previous week. Coming to Michigan with his father before the Civil war, Mr. Allen had settled on the land where he has since lived, clearing it from a dense wilderness. When the rude log home had been complete the mother came on from New York, where the family had previously lived. Mr. Allen is the last of a family of nine children.

John Allen was born in VanBuren township, Onondaga county, New York, December 23, 1825, and was the son of John S. and Permellia Allen and is the last of a family of nine children to pass on. When a young man he came to the locality where he has since lived and there the first log home was built just in front of the more modern home where he died. During the Civil War, after Mr. Allen had enlisted and after he had spent some time in drilling in preparation for leaving for the front within a short time, he went to Illinois to help a brother-in-law, Benj. Hawley, start a new horse power threshing machine which Mr. Hawley had just purchased. While standing on the platform it gave away and Mr. Allen was plunged into the gears below, one leg being so terribly mangled that amputation was necessary. After the leg had healed he went to Chicago where an artificial limb was adjusted but it was not satisfactory and Mr. Allen later constructed one of his own make, a very ingenious affair made of bass wood and with springs and iron which he wore until about three years ago. With this he managed to do his work and go about his duties almost as well as if he had possessed two good limbs.

For a number of years he was in business in Illinois and was township that when people in straightened circumstances were unable to pay their taxes he told them to bring him old rags and junk and these he traded to peddlers in tinware which he in turn sold or traded. This was in war times. Soon after his father was stricken with illness and the son returned to Delhi where he cared for him until his death, his mother making her home with him until her death in 1882 at the age of 83.

December 19, 1872, he was married to Janette Mogle of Eaton county, two children being born to them, Eugene Allen of Dimondale, and Mrs. Parmellia Painter, both of whom survive. Mrs. Allen was a member of the U. B. church at the time of their marriage but both later united with the Free Methodist church. For the past eight years Mr. Allen's mind has been gradually failing, but the spiritual life appeared to grow and become more and more real to him reading the bible, singing and praying often occupying him for hours at a time. Only a few days before his death he repeated almost the entire 51st psalm and often would recite the verses of an old poem which began:

"Don't weep for me, my friends most dear,
I am not dead, but sleeping here;
My debts are paid, my grave is made
Prepare in time to follow me.

Funeral services were held Monday from the home of his daughter, where during his declining year he has been most tenderly cared for. Mr. Allen was one of the few remaining of the older pioneer stock which wrested this rich agricultural region from the dense wilderness of former days. His long life was filled with good deeds and his passing marks the end of a life well lived.

John and Amelia's daughter Martha Allen Holley, Fairmount Cemetery, Denver, Colorado, died age 68.

John and Amelia's daughter Anna Brooks death certificate, died age 70.

John and Amelia's son Elijah Allen, Riverside Memorial Park, Aberdeen, South Dakota, died age 61.

Left: John and Amelia's daughter-in-law Estella Allen, Riverside Memorial Park, Aberdeen, South Dakota. Birth year was actually 1846, died age 44. Estella Doolittle Allen was a twin sister to Ella Doolittle Beebe.
Right: John and Amelia's granddaughter Carrie Allen, Markham Cemetery, Holt, Michigan, died age 13.

John and Amelia's daughter Orisavila Allen Dunn death certificate, died age 82.

John and Amelia's daughter Orisavila Dunn, Lakeview Cemetery, Lakeview, Michigan, died age 82.

~~~

The **1830 US Census** lists John Allen, Onondaga, New York; 1 male child under 5 [John B.]; 1 male child 5-10 [Gilbert]; One male 20-30 [John S.]; 1 female child under 5 [Anne]; 1 female child 5-10 [Eliza]; One female 20-30 [Amelia]

The **1840 US Census** lists John "Allan"; 2 male children under 5 [William H. and Elijah]; 1 male child 10-15 [John B.]; One male 30-40 [John S.]; 1 female child 5-10; 1 female child 10-15; One female 30-40 [Amelia]

The **1850 US Census** lists John "F." Allen 47, farmer, and "Permela" Allen 46, living in Onondaga, New York; Their children [no mention of Gilbert (28), Adeliza was married in 1843, Anne was married in 1847, no mention of Elijah (13)]; John 23; Martha 18; Wm 12; Orsaville 9; George 7

The **1855 New York State Census** lists 9 household members living in Onondaga, New York. John Allen, 50; Pamelia Allen, 49; Elijah Allen, 18; William Allen, 15; George Allen, 9. Also living in the same house were Decatur Paul, 18, cigar maker; Edwin Smiley, 23, cooper; Elizabeth Smiley, 19; Ellen Smiley, 11 months.

The **1860 US Census** lists Amelia (56) living in Delhi, Michigan, with her children: Elijah (23), a farmer, Wm. (21), farm laborer, Orsivilla (19), and George (16). Also listed is John H. Allen (11), relationship unknown. There is no mention of John S. Allen, who would have been 57, living with them. It might be that he had been diagnosed with tuberculosis and was at a hospital for treatment.

The **1870 US Census** lists John and Amelia's son: John Allen, 42, farmer, born New York, living in Ingham County, Michigan; Permelia, 65, keeping home, born New York (her spouse John died in 1864); Unknown relationship: Ella 12 at home, born in Michigan.

The **1880 US Census** lists John Keeler 55, farmer, born New York, living in Alaiedon, Ingham County, Michigan; Eliza Keeler, 55, housekeeper; Eliza and John married in 1870 after her first spouse Gideon's death in 1861; Permelia Allen, 77, mother-in-law, widowed.

~~~

Adeliza "Eliza" Allen Beebe is the Moorman family ancestor. See details in the Maternal Fifth Generation.

~~~

Ebenezer Smith

Born 19 Dec 1797 (Oneida, New York); died 21 Jan 1861 at age 63 (Delhi, Michigan). He married Polly Clark at the age of 26, had his first child at age 26, and his last child at age 38.

> Ebenezer Smith, was Born in 1797 Died in 1861. His wife Polly Clark, Born 1798 Died 1857. Great Grandparents on our Mother's side. Near about 1840 the family moved from Roan N.Y. to Homer Mich. on a farm. 7 Children were Born to this Union, Abagal, Born 1823. Jane-1825. Charles-1827. William-1829. Hellen-1831. Matilda-1833. James-1835.   —From "The Moorman Family"[2]

Left: Ebenezer Smith, 1797–1861, Markham Cemetery, Holt, Michigan, died age 63. Ebenezer and Polly's grandchild, Thelma E. Smith (1852–1856), died 3 years, 8 months, is the small headstone.
Right: Thelma's parents—William H. Smith, 1829–1890, and Mary J. Smith, 1829–1891—are buried on the right side of the small headstone with a larger monument. The small stone (left in picture) says "SISTER." The small stone (right in picture) says "BROTHER."

---

[2] Compiled by Ella Moorman Wood, 1980s, based on Eldora Moorman's materials.

Ebenezer Smith's Ancestors beyond Sixth Generation

7. Ebenezer Smith's parents were **Oliver Smith, Captain** (1752, Hadley, Massachusetts; 30 Mar 1845, Clarendon, New York) and **Abigail Stacy** (5 Mar 1750, Sturbridge, Massachusetts; died before 1820, Onondaga, New York). They married on 26 Apr 1773 (Sturbridge, Massachusetts). Oliver served in the Revolutionary War and later filed for a pension. He was present at Lexington, Massachusetts, on 19 Apr 1775 for the "shot heard round the world." The Smith brothers were part of Ethan Allen's Green Mountain Boys, a militia established in 1770 to fight off people trying to steal land and crops. It later became involved in the Revolutionary War against England.

> "No complete list has been preserved of those who represented Hadley in the Revolution, but we know that Captain Oliver Smith . . . [was] in active service."
> —*Historic Hadley; a Story of the Making of a Famous Massachusetts Town*, p. 66

My Mother Eva Beebe Moornan wrote this little little bit of history of her Mothers Ancestors. (Quote) Mrs. E. [Ellsworth] L. Moorman writes, My Great Great Grandfather [Oliver] Smith, Lived on a farm near Rome N.Y. He fought in the Revolution and togather with 6 other Soldiers escaped from the English war Prison and were forced to eat the mockisons on their feet. and were just casting lots to see which one should be slain to be eat, when they were ruscued. The last year of His life he was totaly blind and lived with his Son Ebenezer. —From "The Moorman Family"

~~~

8. Oliver Smith's parents were **Aaron Smith, Deacon** (7 Feb 1715, Hadley, Massachusetts; 9 Mar 1798, Athol, Massachusetts) and **Abigail Scott** (7 Feb 1715, Hatfield, Massachusetts; 13 May 1769, Athol, Massachusetts). Aaron and Abigail married on 14 Oct 1739 (Hatfield, Massachusetts). They had 7 children. Abigail's father unknown.

Abigail Stacy's parents were **John Stacy Jr.** (22 Aug 1716, Killingly, Connecticut; 1764, Sturbridge, Massachusetts) and **Abigail Allen** (20 Feb 1726/1727, Medfield, Massachusetts; Jun 1801, Sturbridge, Massachusetts). John and Abigail married 1 Nov 1743 (Sturbridge, Massachusetts). John's mother unknown.

~~~

9. Aaron Smith's parents were **Jonathan Smith** (18 Dec 1663, Hadley, Massachusetts; 9 Oct 1737, Hatfield, Massachusetts) and **Abigail Kellogg** (9 Oct 1671, Hadley, Massachusetts; 12 Oct 1741, Hatfield, Massachusetts). Jonathan and Abigail married 14 Nov 1688 (Amherst, Massachusetts). Jonathan's parents unknown.

JONATHAN SMITH, of Hatfield, (Mass.,) was married to Abigail Kellogg, daughter of Joseph Kellogg, of Hadley, in the same State, and of Abigail Kellogg, his second wife, November 14, 1688. She was born Oct 9, 1671. Joseph Kellogg's second wife was Abigail Terry, daughter of Stephen Terry, some time of Hadley, and sister of John Terry, of Simsbury, (Conn.)

Mr. Jonathan Smith died about 1737, aged about 74.

His widow, Mrs. Abigail Smith, died ——.

Children.

3336 Jonathan,	born August	10, 1689.	He lived in Amherst, (Mass.) He had a son Jonathan, who married Rebecca Smith, daughter of Doct. Nathaniel Smith, and he had most of Nathaniel's estate, including a large farm, in the vicinity of where the College now is. He had one daughter and no son.
3337 Daniel,	born March,	3, 1692.	He was crazy.
3338 Abigail,	born April	20, 1695.	
3339 Stephen,	born December	5, 1697.	Lived a while in Amherst, (Mass.)
3340 Prudence,	born May	16, 1700.	
3341 Moses,	born September	8, 1702.	
3342 Elisha,	born July	10, 1705.	Lived in Whately, (Mass.) Married and had 12 children.
3343 Elizabeth,	born May	8, 1708.	
3344 Ephraim,	born March	24, 1711.	Settled in Athol, (Mass.)
3345 Aaron,	born February	7, 1715.	Settled in Athol, (Mass.)

Abigail Scott's mother was **Lydia Leonard** (10 Mar 1679, Hatfield, Massachusetts; 1735, Hatfield, Massachusetts). Lydia's parents unknown.

John Stacy's father was **John Stacy** (7 Nov 1697, Watertown, Massachusetts; Feb 1746, Sturbridge, Massachusetts. John's parents unknown.

Abigail Allen's parents were **Joseph Allen** (17 Aug 1702, Medfield, Massachusetts; 1 Jan 1777, Windham, Connecticut) and **Sarah Parker** (16 Aug 1702, Medfield, Massachusetts; 10 Oct 1760, Norton, Massachusetts). Sarah's mother unknown.

~~~

10. Abigail Kellogg's parents were **Joseph Kellogg** (1 Apr 1626, Great Leighs, England; 27 Jun 1707, Hadley, Massachusetts) and **Abigail Martha Terry** (21 Sep 1646, Windsor, Connecticut; 31 Oct 1726, Northampton, Massachusetts). Joseph and Abigail married 9 May 1667. They had 11 children. Joseph's and Abigail's parents unknown.

Joseph Allen's parents were **Samuel Richard Allen, Deacon** (4 Dec 1660, Bridgewater, Massachusetts; 28 Jun 1750, Bridgewater, Massachusetts) and **Mary** (2 Dec 1660, Bridgewater, Massachusetts; 28 Jul 1727, Bridgewater, Massachusetts). Samuel's and Mary's parents unknown.

Sarah Parker's father was **Jonathan Parker** (18 Jul 1681, Reading, Massachusetts; 16 Jul 1716, Groton, Massachusetts). Jonathan's parents unknown.

~~~

Polly Clark Smith

Born 27 Mar 1798 (New York); died 26 Dec 1857 (Ingham, Michigan) at age 59. Buried Markham Cemetery, Holt, Michigan. Polly married when she was 25, had her first child at age 25, and her last child at age 37. Unable to trace Polly's ancestors.

**Polly Clark Smith, 1798–1857, Markham Cemetery, Holt, Michigan, died age 59.
Small headstone (left) is Polly's granddaughter, Thelma E. Smith. See Ebenezer Smith for details.**

~~~

Ebenezer and Polly Smith Summary

Ebenezer Smith (26) and Polly Clark (25) married about 1823 (location unknown). They had 7 children (all born in New York) in 12 years. The Smiths lived on a farm new Rome, New York. About 1840, they moved to a Homer, Michigan, farm.

> Eva Beebe's Grandmother's Folks, Ebeneezer Smith her great Grandfather (Wife'S name Forgotten [Polly]) There Children Jane Smith Doolittle—James, and William, Wm. was Married to Mary Hilliard. Their Daughter (Thelma) died in Childhood. Hellen Smith married Manning Taylor, three Children— Pearl, Mitalda, and Charlotte all died in Childhood. Charles Smith never Married. also James Smith stayed a bachelor, James is Buried in (Arlington Cemetery) Abigal Smith Married Moses Shaw they had one Daughter and she never Married. —From "The Moorman Family"

1. **Abagail** (1823; ?) married Moses S. Shaw (1812; 1850). They had 1 child: ***Cora*** (1849; ?). Cora never married.

2. **Mary Jane** (1825; 27 Sep 1881, Michigan) married John A. Doolittle (1823; 1888) in 1845. They had 5 children. See details in Maternal Fifth Generation.

3. **Charles** (1827; ?) never married.

4. **William H.** (1829; 1890, Michigan) married Mary J. Hilliard (1829; 1891). They had 1 child: ***Thelma E.*** (1852; 1856) buried next to her parents and grandparents.

5. **Matilda** (1833; ?).

6. **Hellen/Helen** (1835; 1883, Michigan) married Manning B. Taylor (1834; 1866) in 1855. They had 3 children: *Pearlie/Perley/Pearl V.* (1859; 1882), *Alice Matilda "Tillie"* (1863; 1948), *Charlotte* (after 1860 and before 1866; before 1870). In the **1860 US Census,** Stella Doolittle (14), Helen's sister's daughter, was living with the Taylor family in Chickasaw, Iowa. In the **1870 US Census,** Helen (36), a milliner, was living in Grand Rapids, Michigan, with her two daughters. In the **1880 US Census,** Helen (45), a nurse, was living in Lansing, Michigan, with "Tillie" (17). Helen died of cancer.

7. **James** (1835, 1865?, buried Arlington Cemetery, Virginia) never married. A search on the Arlington National Cemetery website resulted in a possible match. James Smith "CIV EMP QMD" died 28 Feb 1865. Buried Section 13, Site 5609.

~~~

Left: Ebenezer and Polly's daughter Helen Smith Taylor, Mount Hope Cemetery, Lansing, Michigan, died age 48. Right: Ebenezer and Polly's son James Smith, Arlington National Cemetery, died age 30.

~~~

Unable to locate the family in the **1830, 1840, 1850 US Census.** In the **1860 US Census,** Ebenezer was 62 and living with John A. Doolittle (36) and Jane Doolittle (33) in Delhi, Michigan, along with John and Jane's daughters Ella (13) and Nellie M. (3). John and Jane's other daughter Stella was living with Helen and Manning Taylor in Iowa.

~~~

Mary Jane Smith Doolittle is the Moorman family ancestor. See details in Maternal Fifth Generation.

~~~

Summary of Maternal Fifth Generation

Gideon Morgan Beebe was born and died (age 45) in Onondaga, New York. Both of his parents died when he was 4 years old. It's unclear who raised him, but he had older brothers and other family members who probably helped care for him.

A family member relates that Morgan was a physician, stonemason, and tailor. However, in the **1850 US Census,** his occupation is listed as "laborer." He married Eliza Allen when he was 27. His first child (Myron Francis) was born when Morgan was 28 and his fourth child was born when Morgan was 36. Morgan is buried in Onondaga Valley Cemetery.

Adeliza "Eliza" Allen Beebe was born in New York and died (at age 76) in Michigan. She married Morgan Beebe in 1843 when she was 19. She gave birth to her first child when she was 21 and to her fourth child when she was 28; that son died age 6 months. Her only daughter died about 17 months later at age 6 years. In the **1860 US Census,** her two other sons were living with relatives in New York.

Morgan died in 1861 at age 45. Eliza married John Keeler (1828; 1905) in 1870 (unknown location). John's death certificate indicates that he died from apoplexy due to alcoholism. He was listed as a "farmhand." Place of burial is listed as Grovenburgh Cemetery, also known as Markham Cemetery.

The **1880 US Census** lists Eliza and John Keeler in Alaiedon, Michigan. Eliza's mother Permelia is living with them. Eliza's son Myron and his family are also living in Michigan. In 1882, at age 59, Eliza Keeler became a member of the RLDS Church. In the **1900 US Census,** John and Eliza are living in Michigan. Her son Myron and his family had moved to Grundy County, Missouri.

Morgan (27) and Eliza (19) married 7 May 1843 (unknown location). They had 4 children in 7 years.

Myron Francis Beebe is the Moorman family ancestor. See details in Maternal Fourth Generation.

John A. Doolittle was born in New York and died (age 65) in Missouri. No details could be located about his parents. He married Jane Smith (in New York) in 1845 (Michigan). His first children (twin girls) were born when he was 23. His last children (twin girls) were born when he was 38. He signed up at the age of 39 to serve in the Civil War. He was later discharged with a medical disability. He was known to be "insane," but there are no specifics about what his mental problems were. Several references list him as a farmer.

It's unknown when John moved to Michigan. The first documentation is his marriage license in 1845, when he was 22. He probably moved to Missouri after his spouse died in 1881. John is buried at the Delano Cemetery in DeKalb County, Missouri.

Jane Smith Doolittle was born in New York and died (age 56) in Michigan. She gave birth to twins at the age of 21. Her last children (another set of twins) were born when she was 36. Out of five children, two died at a young age.

John (22) and Jane (20) married in 1845 (Michigan). They had 5 children in 15 years.

Ella Doolittle Beebe is the Moorman family ancestor. See details in Maternal Fourth Generation.

~~~

Gideon Morgan Beebe

Born 20 Aug 1815 (Onondaga, New York); died 26 Jan 1861 at age 45 (Onondaga, New York). Buried in Onandaga Cemetery, New York.

"Ancestral Chart" lists Gideon as "Physician, stone-mason, men's tailor. Composed songs to sing to his patients."

G. Morgan Beebe, Onondaga Valley Cemetery, Syracuse, New York, died age 45.

~~~

Adeliza "Eliza" Allen Beebe

Born 25 Nov 1824 (Onondaga, New York); died 1900 at age 76 (Holt, Michigan). Buried in Markham Cemetery (Holt, Michigan) under the name "Eliza Allen Keeler."

Baptized and confirmed a member of the RLDS Church in 1882, age 59. Her son Myron had become a member of the RLDS Church in 1877 (in Michigan) at the age of 33.

Eliza was "A lovely little lady with curls about her shoulders. (as I remember her.)"

"My father's mother (Adeliza Keeler when I knew her) was very short and slender. She could stand under my father's outstretched arm." —From "Ancestral Chart"

~~~

Morgan and Eliza Beebe Summary

Gideon Morgan Beebe (27) and Adeliza "Eliza" Allen (19) married 7 May 1843 (location unknown). They had 4 children (all born in New York) in 7 years.

> Gideon Morgan, Son of Mr. Frances, and Eliza Thomas Beebe, were of Scotch decent rom Penn. Gideon M. Beebe, was the Son of a Wealthy Jewleryman, a Native of Penn. On May 1, 1843, Gideon was Married to Eliza Allen. Eliza was the Daughter of John Allen and Permelia Pinckney Allen. Sep 23, 1784. Permelia Pinckney Allen was the Daughter of an Englishman from Novascotia. Mrs. Pinckny was a German Lady from Penn. A Decendent of Ethan Allen of the Revolution. —From "The Moorman Family"

1. **Myron Francis** (4 Jun 1844; 28 Feb 1926, Rosedale, Kansas) married Ella Doolittle (1846; 1890) on 22 Mar 1863 (Ingham County, Michigan). They had 4 children. See details in Maternal Fourth Generation.

2. **Susan Amelia** (3 Jun 1846; 15 Apr 1853, Onondaga, New York) died age 6. Buried Onondaga Valley Cemetery, Syracuse, New York.

3. **Richard Morgan** (12 Aug 1848; 20 May 1925, Long Beach, California) married Catherine "Kate" E. Hadley (1851; 1940) on 6 Sep 1904 (Jackson County, Missouri). No children were born to this marriage, as Kate was 53 years old. In the **1860 US Census,** Richard (12) was living with John (60) and Theresa Pinckney (50) in Onondaga, New York. Richard lived near his brother Myron, who was living with a different Pinckney family. (The Pinckney family was on the brothers' mother's side.) In the **1870 US Census,** Richard (23) lived in San Francisco, California; occupation was listed as a tinsmith. In the **1910 US Census,** Richard and Catherine lived in Los Angeles, California, with a "servant" named Martha Callison (53). In the **1920 US Census,** Richard and Catherine lived in Long Beach, California, along with May Benedict, who was listed as "head" of household and a "pediatrist." The couple was listed as "friend" of May. Richard died of bronchial pneumonia, general arteriosclerosis, and myocarditis. Buried at Sunnyside Cemetery, Long Beach, California.

4. **Lewis John** (7 May 1851; 6 Nov 1851, New York). Buried Onondaga Valley Cemetery, Syracuse, New York, died age 6 months.

Morgan and Eliza's son Richard M. Beebe, Sunnyside Cemetery, Long Beach, California, died age 76.

~~~

In the **1850 US Census,** "Giddeon M. Beebee," 34, is listed as a farmer. His spouse Eliza is 26. They live in Onondaga, New York. Myron is 7, Susan is 4, and Richard is 2.

Unable to locate Morgan or Eliza Beebe in the **1860 US Census.** Their two sons are listed in the **1860 US Census** as living with other families.

Unable to locate Eliza Beebe in the **1870–1900 US Census.**

~~~

Myron Francis Beebe is the Moorman family ancestor. See details in Maternal Fourth Generation.

~~~

John A. Doolittle

Born 1823 (New York, New York); died 25 Dec 1888 at age 65 (DeKalb County, Missouri). Buried Delano Cemetery (DeKalb County, Missouri).

Married Jane Smith 19 Apr 1845 (Clarendon, Michigan). They had 5 children, two sets of twins. His first two daughters (twins) were born when he was 23, and the last two daughters (twins) were born when he was 38.

John A. Doolittle served in the Civil War, enlisting on 30 Dec 1863 (at the age of 39) in Jackson, Michigan. When he registered in Delhi, Michigan, his occupation was listed as "farmer" and his place of birth as "Ohio." Remarks on the document were listed as "said to be insane at times." He was a private in the Union 6th Infantry and was discharged with a disability on 26 Oct 1864.

> Eva Beebe's Mother's Father was John A. Doolittle. He had a bro. Charles, and sister, Mary, one Child Name Forgotten. Married James Lynch. Mary Married a Prior. —From "The Moorman Family"

> The father of Ella Doolittle, John Doolittle, became insane and was kept locked in his room. One day my father [Myron Francis Beebe Sr.] took him with him when he went to tap sugar maples, thinking to give him an outing. After a time father laid down his axe to hang some pails and when he turned around his father-in-law was facing him with the axe held over his head, saying "Now, who's got the battle axe?" Father knew his life was at stake but he calmly looked him in the eye and said, "John, you put that axe down this instant!" After a few harrowing seconds, John put the axe down. And father Beebe took him back and locked him up again. I do not remember whether he recovered or died insane. He was said to have had an uncanny faculty for telling where things were when they were lost anywhere in the house, in spite of the fact he was constantly locked in his room. —From "Ancestral Chart"

Jane died in 1881 and it appears that John moved to DeKalb County, Missouri, to live with/near his daughter Ella and her spouse Myron Francis Beebe. His other living daughter Dora and her spouse James were living in Michigan, according to the **1880 US Census.** They moved to Canada in 1896.

**Left: John A. Doolittle, Delano Cemetery, near Cameron, DeKalb County, Missouri, died age 65.
Right: Jane Smith Doolittle, Markham Cemetery, Holt, Michigan, died age 56.**

~~~

Jane Smith Doolittle

Born 1825 (New York); died 27 Sep 1881 at age 56, cause unknown (Delhi, Michigan). Buried Markham Cemetery (Holt, Michigan). Married John A. Doolittle 19 Apr 1845 (Clarendon, Michigan). They had 5 children, two sets of twins.

> My Grandmother Jane Smith Married John Doolittle.—To this union 5 children were Born. Ella and Estella Twins, 1848. Nellie-1852. Dora and Cora Twins. (My Mother Ella Doolittle) Married Myron Beebe, to this union 4, Children were born. —From "The Moorman Family"

~~~

John and Jane Doolittle Summary

John A. Doolittle (22) and Jane Smith (20) married 19 Apr 1845 (Clarendon, Michigan). They had 5 children, two sets of twins, (all born in Michigan) in 15 years.

1. **Ella** (23 Sep 1846; 6 Jan 1890, DeKalb County, Missouri) married Myron Francis Beebe (1844; 1926) on 22 Mar 1863 (Ingham County, Michigan). They had 4 children. See details in Maternal Fourth Generation.

2. **Estella/Stella** (23 Sep 1846, Ella's twin; 7 May 1891, Aberdeen, South Dakota) married Elijah Allen (1838; 1899) about 1868 (unknown location). They had 4 children: ***Charles I./D.*** (1868; after 1880), ***Ella C.*** (1869; after 1880), ***Carl/Earle E.*** (1873; 1937), ***Oliver G.*** (1877; 1910).

In the **1860 US Census**, Stella Doolittle (14) was living in Iowa with her uncle and aunt, Manning B. and Helen S. Taylor, along with 9-month-old Perlia V. Taylor. In the **1870 US Census**, Stella (23) and Elijah (31) Allen and their 2 children were living with Myron and Ella Beebe (their daughter and son-in-law) and their 2 children in Spring Arbor, Michigan. In the **1885 South Dakota Census**, Stella (35) and Elijah (45) Allen were living in Edmunds County, South Dakota, with their 4 children: Charles, Ella, Carl, Oliver.

3. **Nellie M.** (27 Jun 1857; after 1870).

4. **Dora Polly** (9 Sep 1861; 1 Feb 1942, Edmonton, Alberta, Canada) married James Henry McCue (1849; 1928) in 1880 (Delhi, Michigan). It was his second marriage. They had 3 children: ***Cora Jane*** (1882; 1927), ***Clifford James*** (1883; 1949), ***Adelaide*** (1891; after 1916).

The **1880 US Census** lists James (30) as a farmer and Dora (19) living in Delhi, Michigan. The family moved to Canada in 1896/1897. The **1901 Census of Canada** lists James (52) and Dora (39) as Methodists with children Cora (19), Clifford (17), and Adelaide (10). The **1906 Canada Census** lists James (55), Dara (45), Cara (24), and Adelaide (15). In **May 1910,** James, Dora, and Adelaide (19) crossed the border from Canada to the US at North Dakota, headed for Lansing, Michigan. Clifford was listed as a relative residing in Canada. The **1911 Census of Canada** lists James (62) and Dora (50) with "Adelia" (20) and Wm Emberton (20), a farm laborer. The **1916 Census of Canada** lists James (67) and Dora (55) with Adelaide (25). Dora died age 80; buried Bon Accord, Sturgeon, Alberta, Canada.

5. **Cora** (9 Sep 1861; 20 Apr 1870, Delhi, Michigan) died age 8 due to measles. Buried Cooks Prairie Cemetery, Clarendon, Michigan.

~~~

Left: John and Jane's daughter Dora Doolittle died age 80.
Middle: James McCue died age 79, Bon Accord Cemetery, Sturgeon, Alberta, Canada.
Right: Dau. of J. & J. Doolittle" Cora Doolittle, Cooks Prairie Cemetery, Clarendon, Michigan, died age 8.

~~~

Unable to locate the family in the **1850 US Census.**

The **1860 US Census** lists John (36) as a farmer and Jane (33) living in Delhi, Michigan, with Jane's father, Ebenezer Smith (62). John and Jane's daughters (Ella, 13, and Nellie M., 3) were also listed. In the **1860 US Census**, Stella Doolittle (14) was living in Iowa with M. [Manning] B. and Hellen S. Taylor, along with 9-month-old Perlia [Pearl] V. Taylor. Jane and Helen were sisters, so this was Stella's aunt and uncle.

1860 US Census.

The **1870 US Census** lists John (46) as a farmer and Jane (4) as "keeping home" living in Delhi, Michigan, with daughters Nellie (13) and Dora (9). Cora, Dora's twin, is not mentioned; she died in 1870 at age 8 (measles).

The **1880 US Census** lists John (55) as "insane" and Jane (53) as "keeping house," living in Delhi, Michigan.

~~~

Ella Doolittle Beebe is the Moorman family ancestor. See details in Maternal Fourth Generation.

~~~

Summary of Maternal Fourth Generation

Myron Francis Beebe Sr. was born in New York, then lived in New York, Michigan, Illinois, Missouri. He died in Kansas at the age of 81. He was known as a carpenter, farmer, and dairyman. He married his first spouse Ella Doolittle when he was 18 after moving from New York to Michigan. They had 4 children together in 12 years. He had his first child at the age of 20, and his eighth child (with his second spouse) was born when he was 57. In Michigan, he joined the RLDS Church in 1871 at the age of 27. Ella joined the RLDS Church later that year.

It's uncertain when the family moved from Michigan to Missouri or why they relocated. The **1870 US Census** lists the family living in Michigan. The **1880 US Census** lists the family living in Missouri. Many RLDS members moved to Missouri to be nearer the land they thought of as Zion.

Ella died in 1890 (cause unknown). Her youngest son Harmon was 13. Two years later, in 1892, Myron married Laura Dale Morrison, a single schoolteacher, who was 20 years younger than Myron. They were married in Cameron, Missouri. They had 4 children together in 8 years.

Myron died in Kansas, where he and Laura were living with their daughter Fern and her family. He's buried at Mound Grove Cemetery, Independence, Missouri. There is also a monument with his name on it where his first spouse is buried in Cameron, Missouri.

Myron outlived 6 of his 8 children. One son died just after birth, and another son died age 41 due to accidental poisoning. Myron's grandson, Oscar Myron Moorman (1889; 1963), shares his name.

Ella Doolittle Beebe was born in Michigan. She had a twin sister Estella, who married Elijah Allen. There was another set of twins in the family (Cora and Dora) born in 1861. Dora died age 8 from measles. Cora got married and moved to Canada.

Ella got married when she was 16. She had her first child at age 19. The child only lived for 1 day. She had her fourth child at age 31.

Ella Doolittle (Beebe) was baptized a member of the Reorganized Church of Jesus Christ of Latter Day Saints on 9 July 1871 at Sherman, Michigan, by E. C. Briggs. She was confirmed on 16 July 1871 by E. C. Briggs. She was a Sunday School worker. [Source: Early Reorganization Minutes, 1852-1871, Book A, pp. 749, 910/ Early Reorganization Minutes, 1872-1905, Book C/ Early Reorganization Minutes, 1872-1905, Book E/ Saints' Herald Obituaries, 1890, p. 110]   —From "Ancestral Chart"

Myron F. Beebe, Married Ella Doolittle obout the yead 1864. Ella Doolittle Beebe, Was Born in Calhoun Co. Mich. Sept. 23, 1849 And Died Jan. 6, 1890 at 43 years of age. She is burried in a little Cemetery about 6 miles North of Cameron Mo. Myron F. Beebe was Scotch. Ella Beebe was English. —From "The Moorman Family"

~~~

Eva Beebe Moorman is the Moorman family ancestor. See details in the Maternal Third Generation.

~~~

Myron Francis Beebe Sr.

Myron F. Beebe Sr., Cameron, Missouri.

Born 7 Jun 1844 (Onondaga, New York); died 28 Feb 1926 at age 81 (Rosedale, Kansas).

"Ancestral Chart" lists Myron as a "carpenter, farmer, dairyman. World-wide, -people everywhere, his family and church. Neighborly!"

In the **1860 US Census** Myron (16) is listed as a farm laborer living with Alpheus (26) and Julia (28) Pinckney and their 3-year-old son William in Onondaga, New York. Myron's brother Richard Beebe (12) is listed as living with John (60) and Theresa (50) Pinckney, next door to Alpheus and Julia Pinckney. The Pinckney family was on the brothers' mother's side. Myron's grandmother was Amelia Pinckney, so these couples were related to the boys. It's not known why the boys were living with other families. Their parents Gideon and Eliza cannot be located on the **1860 US Census.** Gideon died in January 1861. In 1863, Myron was in Michigan and married.

Myron married (1) Ella Doolittle. They had 4 children. Myron married (2) Laura Dale Morrison (1864; 1962) on 21 Feb 1892. They had 4 children. Buried Mound Grove Cemetery, Independence, Missouri.

Myron married Ella Doolittle (1846; 1890) on 22 Mar 1863 (Ingham County, Michigan). They had 4 children. **Clarence** (1865; 1865); **Eva Estella** (1868; 1937); **Florence Viola** (1870; 1953); **Harmon Richard** (1877; 1918). See "Myron and Ella Beebe Sr. Summary" for additional details.

Myron was baptized on 11 Feb 1871 at the age of 27 into the Reorganized Church of Jesus Christ of Latter Day Saints (RLDS) in Sherman, Michigan, by Henry C. Smith.

In "Ancestral Chart," there are several references.

Quote from my father (Myron Francis Beebe Sr.):

"The Beebes were all fair of complexion, sandy. All the men were tall-6 feet or over, and slender. Non-religious—Democrats. There were no physical defects and their erect carriage was very noticeable. All were well-educated. They were a high tempered people. My great-grandfather [Samuel Beebe father] came from Scotland."

Quote from Uncle Richard Beebe's letter, dated Aug. 4, 1924.

"Arthur Beebe [Richard's brother] is trying to get the money due us from the Bank of Scotland. They have not given it up yet, but I don't believe we will get it. We have relatives in England who are working on it. They may work it out but I don't believe it!" (They didn't-ha!)

Quote: From a Rochester, N.Y. paper of June 19, 1924.

"The recent passing away of Jim Beebe [1868; 1924, son of Wallace and Mary Beebe], the well-known left-handed violinist of Syracuse, at the County Hospital, of paralysis, recalls to the writer's mind pleasing events that happened years ago. Jim was a marvel with his violin and many a night us kids would linger around his studio and hear Chase [Susan Beebe's spouse?] and Beebe rattle off the famous pieces that were the go in those days. — He not only could produce marvelous tone upon his fiddle but he was capable of making it sing, and how he could make the bow jump up and down. Jim was very clever in doing a great many tricks upon his instrument, but he is gone"— etc. — by Thomas W. Crumm.

Uncle Richard [Beebe] knew Jim and his relationship to him and my father [Myron Francis Beebe Sr.]. He sent the clipping to my father. Jim was probably the grandson of Lawrence or Richard—grandfather [Gideon Morgan] Beebe's brothers.

After Myron's first spouse Ella died in Jan 1890, Myron married **Laura Dale Morrison** (1864; 1962) on 21 Feb 1892 (Cameron, Missouri). See additional details after Ella Doolittle section.

Myron is buried at Mound Grove Cemetery (Independence, Missouri) next to his second spouse Laura. However, there is also a monument with his name at Delano Cemetery (Cameron, Missouri) where Ella is buried.

~~~

Ella Doolittle Beebe

Born 23 Sep 1846 (Clarendon, Calhoun County, Michigan); died 6 Jan 1890 at age 43 (unknown cause, probably died near Cameron, Missouri). Buried at Delano Cemetery (Cameron, Missouri).

Left: Ella Doolittle Beebe. Middle and right, Delano Cemetery, DeKalb County, Missouri, died age 43.

Ella Doolittle (Beebe) was baptized a member of the Reorganized Church of Jesus Christ of Latter Day Saints on 9 July 1871 at Sherman, Michigan, by E. C. Briggs. She was confirmed on 16 July 1871 by E. C. Briggs. She was a Sunday School worker. [Source: Early Reorganization Minutes, 1852-1871, Book A, pp. 749, 910/ Early Reorganization Minutes, 1872-1905, Book C/ Early Reorganization Minutes, 1872-1905, Book E/ Saints' Herald Obituaries, 1890, p. 110]   —From "Ancestral Chart"

Myron F. Beebe, Married Ella Doolittle about the yead 1864. Ella Doolittle Beebe, Was Born in Calhoun Co. Mich. Sept. 23, 1849 [sic] And Died Jan. 6, 1890 at 43 years of age. She is burried in a little Cemetery about 6 miles North of Cameron Mo.   —From "The Moorman Family"

~~~

Myron and Ella Beebe Sr. Summary

Myron Francis Beebe (18) and Ella Doolittle (16) married on 22 Mar 1863 (Ingham County, Michigan). They had 4 children in 12 years. Myron's mother (Eliza Allen Beebe) was a sister to Ella's father (Elijah Allen). Eliza and Elijah's parents were John and Amelia Allen, so Myron and Ella shared one set of grandparents.

Myron was 20 when his first child was born and 57 when his last child was born (with his second spouse Laura). Ella was 19 when her first child was born and 31 when her last child was born. The first 3 children were born in Michigan (upper and central Michigan), while the 4th child was born near Chicago, Illinois. It's unknown why they were in Illinois at that time. A few years later, the family was living in Missouri.

Eva was born near Sugar Grove, Mason County, Michigan. Florence was born in Springport township, Jackson County, Michigan, and Harmon in Wheaton, DuPage County, Illinois. —From "Ancestral Chart"

When Ella died in 1890, her 3 living children were ages 22 to 13. Florence and Eva had married in 1887 and 1888, leaving Harmon at home with his dad at age 13. In 1892, Myron married Laura.

"This is the old M. F. Beebe Home place at Cameron Mo. Myron F. Beebe His wife Ella Doolittle Beebe, Harmon there last Child and his pet Squirl." —From "The Moorman Family"

1. **Clarence** (7 May 1865, Michigan; 8 May 1865, Michigan). Died one day old of unknown cause.

2. **Eva Estella** (10 Jun 1868, Sugar Grove, Michigan; 17 Oct 1937, Knob Noster, Missouri) married Ellsworth L. Moorman (1868; 1948) on 18 Feb 1888 (Cameron, Missouri). They had 6 children. See details in Maternal Third Generation.

3. **Florence Viola** (21 Jul 1870, Springport, Michigan; 23 Jan 1953, Bellflower, California). Buried under the name of Florence Moorman at Rose Hills Memorial Park (Whittier, California). Married (1) John Moorman (1866; 1935) on 29 May 1887 (Cameron, Missouri). They had 3 children: ***Roscoe Francis*** (1888; 1942), ***Maud M.*** (1892; 1895), ***Oral*** (1894; 1894). Maud died age 3 and Oral died age 5 months. They are buried in a cemetery

about six miles north of Cameron, Missouri. Florence and John separated about 1900. Eva and Florence (sisters) married brothers (Ellsworth and John).

Florence married (2) mechanical engineer Albert "Bert" Wilson Mount (1877; 1955) in 1902 in Ontario, Canada, when both were 25 years old. Florence and Bert divorced in 1918. The **1920 US Census** shows Florence Mount as married and head of household. Living with her are daughter Lila Mount (14) and granddaughter Ana Jean Moorman (1) living in Washington, Missouri, next to M. F. and Laura D. Beebe. The **1930 US Census** shows Florence as widowed living with her son Roscoe (41), her daughter-in-law Myrtle (32), and her grandson John A. (5) in Sedalia, Missouri.

Roscoe Francis Beebe

John and Florence's son **Roscoe Francis Beebe** married (1) Mildred Elizabeth Schwartz Gill (1899; 1981). They had 1 child: Anna Jean Beebe Chapman (1918; 1984). John and Mildred divorced. Roscoe married (2) Myrtle Bugbee (1898; 1972) on 15 Aug 1920 (Knob Noster, Missouri). They had 1 child: John "Jack" M. Allen (1924; 1994). Roscoe, a conductor and brakeman, died of an "acute coronary occlusion" at 2 A.M. on a Missouri Pacific freight train en route from Jefferson City to Kansa City. Roscoe is buried in Knob Noster Cemetery, Missouri.

> Roscoe loved Playing His Violin, and Piano. He was a Master on the Violin. Was an Elder in the Church. A wonderful Husband, and Father. He Loved Railroading. Was a Conductor, on the Mo. Pacific R.R. Music, and His Home was His Hobby. —From "The Moorman Family"

Lila Blake Mount Barth Hungerford

Florence and Bert adopted **Lila Blake Mount Barth Hungerford** (1905; 1995) who married (1) Webster Ewing Barth (1890; 1965) in 1923 (Manhattan, New York). Lila and Webster had 2 children: Merle Blake (1923; 1944) and Barbara June Barth (1928; 1995). Lila (66) married (2) Arthur W. Hungerford (78) in 1971 (Los Angeles, California). Lila died in Los Angeles and is buried in Rose Hills Memorial Park, Whittier, California.

Lila and Webster's son Merle enlisted "for the duration of the War" (World War 2) on 3 Feb 1942 as a private in the US Army Air Force and attained the rank of first lieutenant. He was reported missing in action on 20 Nov 1944 in England. Merle was a pilot and bailed out of his airplane after it was on fire, likely due to mechanical failure. It was later determined that he had been killed in action and buried at sea. He was awarded the Air Medal with 4 Oak Leaf Clusters.

4. Harmon Richard (2 Jan 1877, Wheaton, Illinois; 28 Jul 1918, Benton County, Missouri) married Ethel Cordelia Manlove (1881; 1948) on 25 Aug 1897 (St. Joseph, Missouri). They had 3 children: **Ivan Earl** (1899; 1928), **Finis Devillo** [Devillo was Ethel's father's first name] (1901; 1970), **Dale Harmon** (1917; 1998). Dale was in the US Navy, World War II, petty officer, third class. Harmon Richard died age 41 from "accidental gas poisoning from well." Ivan died age 49 when he was "crushed by falling rock in a coal mine at Napoleon Mo."

~~~

Left: Myron and Ella's daughters Florence and Eva Beebe, Ludington, Michigan.
Middle: Myron and Ella's daughter Florence and spouse John Moorman.
Right: Myron and Ella's grandchildren, Florence and John's children: "Roscoe and little Sister Maud Moorman."

San Leandroan Aids In Destructive Raid

Homeward bound from a bomber escort mission over Germany, Lieut. Merle B. Barth, of 838 Joaquin Avenue, San Leandro, took time out to share in the destruction of a locomotive and to riddle an armed corvette.

The 20-year-old Mustang flier is based at an Eighth-Air Force Fighter station in England.

"I made two passes at the moving locomotive, both times observing many hits in the boiler," he reported.

Of the armed corvette off the Dutch coast, he said, "My slugs were ripping into the bow of the vessel and she appeared to sink as I pulled up."

23 NOVEMBER 1944.

ON 20 NOVEMBER 1944 LT. MERLE B. BARTH CALLED ON THE R/T AND SAID "COOKIE, I'M GOING TO GET OUT OF HERE I AM ON FIRE." HE PEELED OFF OUT OF FORMATION AT 16,000 FT. AND I PEELED OFF AFTER HIM. I LOST HIM IN THE OVERCAST SO I DROPPED DOWN UNDER THE CLOUDS TO SEE IF I COULD FIND HIM BUT HE DID NOT COME DOWN. I THEN SWITCHED TO "B" CHANNEL BUT DID NOT HERE ANYTHING SO I SWITCHED TO "A" CHANNEL AND CALLED MY FLIGHT LEADER, LT. HUNTER, AND TOLD HIM I HAD LOST BARTH IN THE OVERCAST. HE TOLD ME TO COME BACK AND JOIN FORMATION. I HEARD LT. HUNTER TRANSMITTING FOR A FIX.

BOYD N. ADKINS JR,
F/O, AIR CORPS.

Left: 20 Oct 1944 *Oakland Tribune*, Oakland, California: Right: 23 Nov 1944 report about Merle Barth.

3. Description of extent of damage to missing aircraft (includ fires, explosions, etc):

Lt. Barth was heard saying his A/C was on fire, and in his last message to the controller said his cockpit was so filled with smoke that he would have to bail out.

4. If aircraft was out of control describe appearance:

Lt. Barth apparently had good control of his A/C during the time he was attempting to return to base.

Report about Merle Barth.

Myron and Ella's daughter and grandson. Left: "Flo and Roscoe." Middle: "Roscoe Playing His Violin." Right: Roscoe.

Myron and Ella's grandson Roscoe Francis Moorman Draft Registration Card, 1917.

Left: "Roy and Ella Wood, Erwin, Roscoe & Oscar Moorman."
Middle: "Roscoe and His Father Holding Jack his Grandchild." Right: "Roscoe and Daughter Anna Jean."

Left: Myron and Ella's granddaughter Anna Jean. Middle: Anna Jean and her grandmother Flo.
Right: "Roscoe, Roma, Ella, Flo, Sis, [front:] Eddie and Pat Guy."

"Kay Moorman, Jack and Florence Guy, Roscoe, Anna Jean and Flo Moorman, Stella Hines and dog."

Myron and Ella's grandson Roscoe Moorman, Knob Noster, Missouri, died age 53.

Myron and Ella's grandson Roscoe Moorman, Knob Noster, Missouri, death certificate, died age 53.

Left: Aunt Flo, Barbara, Webster, Lila Barth. Middle: Webster, Barbara, Merle Barth.
Right: Barbara Barth, Anna Jean Moorman, and Lila Barth. Virginia Dungan photo.

Left: Myron and Ella's grandson Finis Devillo (actual burial is in Gravette, Arkansas—see image on right),
grandson Ivan Earl died age 28, Ethel Cordelia died age 67, and son Harmon Richard died age 41, Knob Noster
Cemetery, Missouri. Third grandson Dale Harmon buried in Bay Pines National Cemetery, Florida, died age 81.
Right: Myron and Ella's grandson Finis D. Beebe, Hillcrest Cemetery, Gravette, Benton County, Arkansas, died
age 69. His spouse's family was from Arkansas.

Myron and Ella's son "Herman" Harmon R. Beebe death certificate.

Myron and Ella's grandson Ivan E. Beebe death certificate.

Myron and Ella's children Harmon and Eva, Cameron, Missouri, 1897.

~~~

In the **1920 US Census,** Florence Mount (status married and head of family), her daughter Lila (14), and her granddaughter Anna Jean Moorman (1 yr and 7 mo) lived next to Myron and Laura Beebe.

In the **1930 US Census,** Florence Mount (status widowed), was living with her son Roscoe F. Moorman (41) listed as a conductor for a steam railroad, his spouse Myrtle, and their son John A. Moorman (5) in Sedalia, Missouri.

In the **1930 US Census,** Webster E. Barth (39), listed as a newspaper circulator, and Lila B. (25) are living with Merle B. (6) and Barbara J. (21 months) living in Oakland, California.

~~~

Laura Dale Morrison Beebe, Myron's second wife

Laura was born 16 Oct 1864 (Delaware County, Ohio); died 13 Mar 1962 at age 96 of arteriosclerotic heart disease (Independence, Missouri). She was a schoolteacher, 20 years younger than Myron. They had 4 children.

Laura is the grandmother that Virginia Moorman Dungan knew. Virginia wrote more often about the children of Myron and Laura, especially Virginia's Great-Aunt Fern and Great-Uncle Ray Lloyd, along with Great-Aunt Alta May Beebe Hamilton.

Laura Dale Morrison and Myron Beebe. Married Cameron, Missouri, Feb 1892.

Left: Laura Dale Morrison Beebe, location and date unknown.
Right: Laura D. died age 96 and Myron F. Beebe died age 81, Mound Grove Cemetery, Independence, Missouri.

1. **Jennie Fern Beebe Lloyd** (1892; 1991) married Joseph Ray Lloyd (1887; 1962) on 28 Dec 1913 (Knob Noster, Missouri). Both are buried at Mound Grove Cemetery (Independence, Missouri). They had one daughter *Mildred Lorene Lloyd* (1914; 2000).

2. **Alta May Beebe Hamilton** (1897; 1988) married Duke Lee Hamilton (1890; 1970) on 28 Oct 1919 (location unknown). Alta is buried at Mount Olive Cemetery (Bolivar, Missouri). They had 5 children. *Duke Lee Jr.* (1920; 1943), *Cecil Allen* (1923; 2001), *Dorothy Anne* (1925; 2007), *Frederick Dale* (1927; 2013), *Myron Alexander* (1928; 2010).

Duke Jr. was in the Army Air Forces in World War 2 as a B-17 flight engineer. His plane was shot down over Brittany, France. He received a Purple Heart.

> During World War II the "Flying Fortress"—B-17, was shot down with the crew and Duke, Jr. and others— all were seen to parachute out but none survived, Jan. 23, 1943.   —From "Ancestral Chart"

3. Myron Francis Beebe Jr. (1900; 1963) married (1) Clara Richmond Bennett (1902; 1965) in 1925 (Pennsylvania), one stepson Basil (1920; ?). Myron and Clara divorced before 1940. Myron married (2) Thelma Loreen Lupton James (1911; 1991) on 10 Dec 1939 (Independence, Missouri). The **1940 US Census** shows Myron living in California with Thelma and stepson Richard Lee James (1935; ?). Myron was a cement finisher; died of lung cancer.

4. Cecil Dale Beebe (1901; 1996) married Frances Roma Moorman (1906; 2002) on 29 Sep 1924 (Independence, Missouri). Roma's father was Eugene Moorman, son of Edwin and Mahala Jane Moorman. Eugene's brother Ellsworth married Eva Beebe, Cecil's half-sister. They had 2 children: ***Myron Eugene*** (1925; ?), ***Cecil Ray*** (1929; 1999). Cecil was a retired court reporter, having worked for many years in American Samoa and Honolulu, Hawaii.

~~~

Front: A Joyful Christmas

 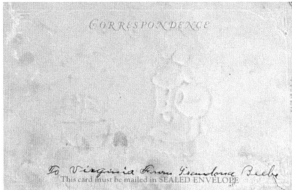

Postmark: none [after 1920, before 1962]

To: Virginia From Grandma Beebe [Laura Dale Morrison Beebe (1864-1962)]

Editor Note: This card dates to the 1900-1920 era. It's an embossed linen type heavy card stock. The back says "Correspondence" and "This card must be mailed in SEALED ENVELOPE." In smaller print, on the right side, is written "MADE IN U.S.A."

~~~

Left: "Aunt Fern, Daddy's 1/2 Aunt, Sister to Fern Lloyd Cecil Beebe, daughter, Grandma Beebe." Dec 1972, location unknown. Virginia Dungan photo.
Right: Fern died age 98 and Ray Lloyd died age 74, Mound Grove Cemetery, Independence, Missouri.

Left: Duke and Alta May Beebe Hamilton. Middle: "Alta Hamilton with Helen Moorman."
Right: Alta died age 90 and Duke died age 80, Mount Olive Cemetery, Bolivar, Missouri.

Left: Duke and Alta's son Duke Lee Hamilton Jr.
Right: Duke and Alta's son Allen Hamilton, age 19, US Army Air Force, World War 2.

Left: Duke and Alta's son Freddie holding David, first spouse Kathalee holding Laura.
Right: Duke and Alta's son Myron A. Hamilton.

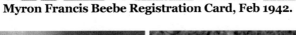

Myron Francis Beebe Jr. Registration Card, Sep 1918.

Myron Francis Beebe Registration Card, Feb 1942.

Left: Beebe family, possibly Myron and Laura with their son Cecil Dale Beebe and child.
Right: Myron and Laura's son Cecil Dale Beebe, Humansville Cemetery, Missouri, died age 94.

Standing left to right: Cecil Beebe, Harry Moorman, Finis Beebe, Ernest Moorman, Ellsworth Moorman, Myron Beebe. Kneeling left to right: Roy Wood, Erwin Moorman. Knob Noster, Missouri, circa 1946. Virginia Dungan photo. Cecil and Myron are brothers. Ernest and Ellsworth are brothers. Ellsworth's sons are Harry and Erwin and his son-in-law is Roy. Finis's father was Harmon, half-brother to Cecil and Myron.

~~~

In the **1870 US Census,** Myron Beebe (26) had moved to Spring Arbor, Michigan, and was living with his spouse Ella (23) and two children (Eva E., 2, and Florence V., 1 month). Myron and Ella lived next door to Elijah and Estella Allen and their two children. Estella and Ella were sisters.

In the **1880 US Census,** M. F. Beebe (36) and Ella (33) were living in Grand River, Missouri, with Eva (11), Florence (9), and Harmon (3).

Unable to locate family in **1890 US Census.** Most of these records were destroyed in a fire at the Commerce Department Building in January 1921.

In the **1900 US Census,** Myron F. Beebe (55) and Laura D (35) were living in Spickardville, Franklin Township, Grundy County, Missouri, with Fern (7), Alta (4), and Myron F. (4 mo.).

In the **1910 US Census,** Myron F. Beebe (65) listed as a dairyman on a home farm and Laura D. (45) were living in Washington Township, Johnson County, Missouri, with Fern (17), Alta (12), Myron F. (10), and Cecil D. (9).

In the **1920 US Census,** M. F. Beebe (75) listed as a "cream tester" and Laura D. (55) were living in Washington, Missouri, with Myron F. (20). Myron and Ella's daughter Florence Mount lived next door with her daughter and granddaughter.

In the **1925 Kansas Census,** Myron F. (80) listed as a carpenter and Laura D. (60) were living in Wyandotte County, Kansas, with son-in-law Ray (37) and daughter Fern (32) Lloyd and their daughter Lorene (10). Ray worked for Health Analysis Int.

In the **1930 US Census,** Laura B. Beebe (65), widow, was living with Joseph R. Lloyd (43) a sales manager at a business school, Fern (37), and Mary A. (5) in Kansas City, Kansas.

In the **1940 US Census,** Laura B. Beebe (75) was living with Joseph R. Lloyd (53) a teacher salesmanship and Jenni (47) in Kansas City, Kansas.

~~~

Eva Beebe Moorman is the Moorman family ancestor. See details in the Maternal Third Generation.

~~~

Summary of Maternal Third Generation

Eva Estella Beebe Moorman was born in Sugar Grove, Sherman Township, Mason County, Michigan (about 100 miles north of Grand Rapids and 10 miles east of Lake Michigan), as the second of four siblings. Her older brother Clarence had died in 1865 (3 years before Eva was born) when he was one day old. Her parents had been married in Ingham County, Michigan, near Lansing (located in the middle of Michigan). It's unknown why the family was in Mason County in 1868. Two years later, Eva's sister Florence was born in Springport, Jackson County, Michigan, which is south of Lansing. In 1877, Eva's brother Harmon was born in Wheaton, Illinois, a suburb of Chicago. The family moved to Missouri after 1877 and before June 1880, when the **1880 US Census** shows the family living in Grand River Township, DeKalb County, Missouri. DeKalb County is an area located between St. Joseph and Cameron, Missouri.

Eva (19) married Ellsworth (19) on 18 Feb 1888 in Cameron, Missouri. Her mother Ella Doolittle Beebe died in 1890 when Eva was 22. Her father Myron Francis Beebe Sr. married Laura Dale Morrison Beebe in 1890. Myron and Laura had 4 children, who were Eva's stepsiblings, although she was not raised in the same household with them. Eva and Ellsworth had 6 children over a span of 18 years. She had her first child, Oscar, at the age of 21. She had her last child, Florence, at the age of 39. Out of 6 children, 5 lived to be adults. Her son William Oral was born in Osceola, Iowa, and died age 1 year and 2 months, cause unknown. He is buried in Murray Cemetery, Murray, Iowa. All the other children were born in Missouri, including Cameron, Laredo (north central part of Missouri), and Washington (Township, Knob Noster, Johnson County). Oscar Myron (1889; 1963), Erwin Everett (1892; 1990), Ella Neosho (1894; 1966), William Oral (1899; 1900), Harry Ellsworth (1904; 1962), and Florence Geneva (1907; 2003).

After Eva moved from Michigan to Missouri, it appears that she lived the rest of her life in Missouri. However, she might have lived in Iowa about 1900 because one of her children is buried there. Her death certificate indicates that she lived that last 20 years of her life (1917; 1937) in Knob Noster, Missouri. Eva died in 1937 in Knob Noster, Missouri, at the age of 69. Her death certificate lists the cause of death as cirrhosis of liver, infectious nonspecific. Contributory causes are listed as cholelithiasis and arteriosclerosis. She's buried at Knob Noster Cemetery in Missouri. She was survived by her spouse and five of her six children. Ellsworth lived for nine more years, marrying Minnie "Mickey" Hutchens Scott (1879; 1969) on 3 Mar 1940 (Knob Noster, Missouri).

Eva's children lived to be from 58 to 98 years old. Oscar's cause of death was pulmonary infarction, myocardial infarction mural thrombus, coronary atherosclerosis with occlusion. The other causes of death are unknown—online historical access to Missouri death certificates is limited to records more than 50 years old.

Eva (19) married Ellsworth (19) in 1888 (Cameron, Missouri). They had 6 children in 18 years.

~~~

Oscar Myron Moorman is the Moorman family ancestor. See details in the Paternal Second Generation.

~~~

Eva Estella Beebe Moorman

Born 10 Jun 1868 (Sherman/Sugar Grove, Mason County, Michigan); died 17 Oct 1937 at age 69 (Knob Noster, Missouri). Buried Knob Noster Cemetery (Knob Noster, Missouri). Married Ellsworth L. Moorman (1868; 1948) on 18 Feb 1888 (Cameron, DeKalb County, Missouri). Ellsworth Moorman's details and a summary of Eva and Ellsworth are given under "Paternal Moorman Family." The 6 children of Eva and Ellsworth are listed after this information in the "Summary of Maternal/Paternal Second Generation."

Eva Beebe Moorman. Knob Noster Cemetery, Missouri, died age 69.

Eva Beebe Moorman.

Eva E. Beebe Moorman, death certificate

In the **1870 US Census,** Eva (2) is living in Spring Arbor, Michigan, with her parents Myron (26) listed as a farmer and Ella (23) listed as a boarder and sister Florence (1 month).

In the **1880 US Census,** Eva (11) is living in Grand River Township, DeKalb County, Missouri, with her parents M. F. (36) listed as a farmer and Ella (33) listed as keeping house and sister Florence (9) and brother Harmon (3).

~~~

Paternal Moorman Family

Color Coding for Moorman Paternal Ancestors

The following color coding has been used to help readers trace the generations.

First generation: parents, aunts, uncles
Second generation: grandparents, great-aunts, great-uncles
Third generation: great-grandparents
Fourth generation: great-great-grandparents
Fifth generation
Sixth generation

Virginia Moorman's father was Oscar Myron Moorman.

Oscar Moorman's father was Ellsworth L. Moorman.

Ellsworth L. Moorman's parents were Edwin and Mahala "Hallie" Jane Elwood Moorman.

Edwin Moorman's parents were William and Katherine "Kitty" Winston Johnson Moorman.

Hallie Elwood's parents were George Washington and Narcissa Shockley Elwood.

William Moorman's parents were Charles and Elizabeth "Betty" Johnson Moorman.

Kitty Johnson's parents were Joseph Ellison and Agatha Agnes Moorman Johnson.

George Washington Elwood's parents were Henry Shaw and Sarah Sinclair Elwood.

Narcissa Shockley's parents were Benjamin and Sally Melson Shockley.

~~~

Summary of Paternal Sixth Generation and Beyond

Charles Moorman traced to the 15th generation in 1510 with ancestors from England, Scotland, and Virginia, including titles of Lady, Sir, Earl, Countess, Captain, Lt. Col, and Doctor (one doctor created a secret remedy of aurum potabile). One ancestor was imprisoned by the Spanish and later ransomed by King James I. One ancestor was a pilot on the *Mayflower*, with several ancestors settling in the original Jamestown, Virginia, as part of the Virginia Land Company. Several castles and houses in England were part of this family heritage. One castle is a tourist site.

Elizabeth "Betty" Johnson Moorman traced to the 15th generation in 1510—the same as Charles Moorman; Charles and Betty shared the same grandparents. Charles (21) and Betty (20), both Quakers, married in 1788 (Virginia). They had 9 children in 19 years. Their children served in the Civil War (Union) and occupations were shoemaker, mill sawyer, tin maker, carder, engineer, peddler, waiter, carpenter, painter, laborer, lawyer, nurseryman, gunsmith, seamstress, farmer, fanning, and clerking.

William Moorman is the Moorman family ancestor. See details in the Paternal Fifth Generation.

~~~

Joseph Ellison Johnson traced to the 9th generation with ancestors in Scotland and Virginia. Several of the Johnson family were Quakers. Many were pioneer settlers in Virginia.

Agatha Agnes Moorman Johnson. Agatha's father and Charles Moorman's father (see above) were brothers, so this made them cousins. Follow Charles's ancestors later in this section. Joseph (21) and Agatha (17) married in 1785 (Virginia). They had 9 children in 19 years.

Katherine "Kitty" Winston Johnson Moorman is the Moorman family ancestor. See details in the Paternal Fifth Generation.

~~~

Henry Shaw Elwood traced to the 7th generation in 1751. Henry was born in 1789 in Pennsylvania to parents who were both born in Ireland. His mother died the day he was born. It's unknown when the family moved to

Ohio. Henry married in Ohio in 1814. Henry's father might have been an alcoholic, or at least had challenges with alcohol that created a problem in 1818, the year he died. Henry's children were born in Ohio from 1817 to 1840. In 1849, the family moved to Iowa, where Henry died in 1863.

Sarah Sinclair Elwood traced to the 13th generation in 1620, with ancestors from England, Netherlands, Delaware, Kentucky, New Jersey, New York, North Carolina, and Virginia. Ancestors served in the US Revolutionary War, the War of 1812, and the US Civil War. Sarah was born in 1798 in Kentucky. It's unknown when the family moved to Ohio where Sarah was married in 1816. She gave birth to all her children in Ohio. In 1849, the family moved to Iowa, where Sarah died in 1866. Henry Shaw Elwood (26) and Sarah Sinclair (18) married in 1816 (Ohio). They had 10 children in 23 years.

George Washington Elwood is the Moorman family ancestor. See details in the Paternal Fifth Generation.

~~~

Benjamin Shockley traced to the 10th generation in 1620 with ancestors in England and Maryland.

Sally Melson Shockley traced to 12th generation in 1621 with ancestors in England, Delaware, Maryland, and Virginia. Ancestors served in the Civil War on the Union side. Benjamin (23) and Sally (16) married in 1804 (Maryland). They had 19 children in 28 years.

Narcissa Shockley Elwood is the Moorman family ancestor. See details in the Paternal Fifth Generation.

~~~

Moorman Paternal Ancestors

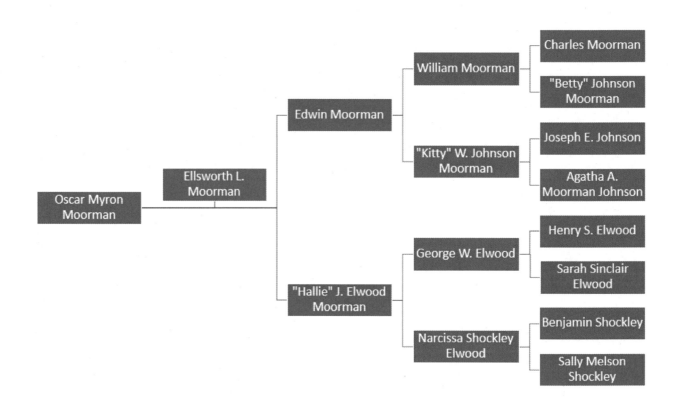

Moorman Paternal Family Ancestor Locations

Oscar Myron Moorman Paternal Family Locations

Maryland, Manokin, 1677: Shockley ancestors (Mahala Jane's mother's family) (near Delmar, Delaware, and east of Chesapeake Bay)

Virginia, Green Spring, 1705: Moorman ancestors (Edwin family) (northern border near West Virginia)

Delaware, Delmar, 1730: Sarah Shockley ancestors (near Manokin, Maryland)

Maryland, Worcester County, 1780: Benjamin/Sarah Shockley, Narcissa's grandparents (near Manokin)

Virginia, Lynchburg, 1792: William Moorman birth, Oscar's great-grandfather (30 miles from Bedford)

Virginia, Bedford, 1798: Kitty Winston Johnson birth, Oscar's great-grandmother (30 miles from Lynchburg)

Ohio, Martinsville, 1817: George Washington Elwood birth, Oscar's great-grandfather (12 miles from Highland)

Ohio, Highland, 1824: Narcissa Shockley birth, Oscar's great-grandmother (12 miles from Martinsville)

Ohio, Highland, 1832: Edwin Moorman birth, Oscar's grandfather

Ohio, 1842: George and Narcissa (wife 1) marriage

Ohio, Martinsville, 1844; Ohio, 1846: Mahala "Hallie" Jane Elwood birth; death, Oscar's grandmother

Iowa, Henry County, 1847-1849: Narcissa Shockley's parents' deaths (Mount Pleasant, ~50 miles north of Nauvoo, Illinois)

Iowa, 1850: G. W. Elwood and Sarah Ann Botts (wife 2) had son

Iowa, Des Moines, 1860: Warren, 1870: G. W. and Sarah Elwood, US Census

Iowa, Pleasant Plain, 1862: Edwin and Mahala Jane Elwood Moorman marriage (30 miles from Mount Pleasant)

Missouri, Butler, 1868: Ellsworth L Moorman birth (70 miles south of Independence)

Iowa, Prairie City, 1870: Mahala Jane, US Census (20 miles east of Des Moines)

Iowa, Pleasant Plain, 1870: William Moorman death

Iowa, Richland, 1870; Palmyra, 1880: Edwin and Mahala Jane Moorman, US Census (35 miles from Mount Pleasant)

Iowa, Jefferson County, 1874: Kitty Winston Johnson Moorman death (Pleasant Plain)

Iowa, Prairie City, 1877: George Elwood death

Missouri, Cameron, 1888: Ellsworth and Eva Estella Beebe Moorman marriage (50 miles from Independence)

Missouri, Knob Noster, 1909: Edwin Moorman death

Missouri, Washington, 1910: E L and Eva Moorman (Edwin and Mahala Jane's son)

Missouri, Knob Noster, 1922: Mahala Jane Elwood death (about 65 miles from Independence)

Missouri, Knob Noster, 1930-1948: Ellsworth and Eva Moorman

Charles Moorman

Born 8 Jan 1767, South River, Bedford, Virginia; died 3 Oct 1823 at age 56, Fairfield County, Ohio; "buried James Johnson's on Fall Creek." Charles Moorman was a Quaker. At the age of 21, Charles married Elizabeth "Betty" Johnson, also a Quaker, on 2 Dec 1788 in Amelia County, Virginia. Charles and Betty shared the same grandparents (Thomas and Rachel Moorman). Charles and Betty had 9 children from 1792 to 1811. His son William Moorman was born in 1792 when Charles was 25. His last child was born in 1811 when Charles was 44.

On 20 Dec 1788, Charles was "disowned" from the Quaker faith for "marrying contrary to discipline and to a near relative." On 17 Sep 1791, Charles complained about his "going out in marriage" and requested reinstatement. On 11 Jun 1796, Charles complained of misconduct and was accepted back into the faith. In 1806, the family transferred to the Miami Quaker group in Ohio.

Charles Moorman's Ancestors beyond Sixth Generation

7. Charles Moorman's parents were **Micajah Moorman** (28 Jun 1735, Green Springs, Louisa County, Virginia; 25 Nov 1806, Campbell County, Virginia; buried in Seneca Graveyard, Jamestown, Greene County, Ohio) and **Susanna Chiles** (7 Aug 1738, Caroline County, Virginia; 15 Apr 1782, Bedford County, Virginia; buried Seneca Graveyard, Jamestown, Greene County, Ohio). Micajah and Susannah, both Quakers, married on 13 Oct 1754 (Green Spring Quaker Meeting House, Louisa County, Virginia). They had 13 children from 1755 to 1782. They sold 210 acres on Ivey Creek, Bedford County, September 28, 1778.

~~~

8. Micajah Moorman's parents were **Thomas Moorman** (14 Sep 1705, Green Springs, Louisa County, Virginia; 10 Nov 1767, "a worthy member" (Quaker), Lynchburg, Campbell County, Virginia, buried in South River Quaker Cemetery, Lynchburg, Virginia) and **Rachel Clark,** later Ballard (14 Jun 1714, New Kent, Hanover County, Virginia; 10 Jun 1792, Bedford, Lynchburg, Virginia, buried in South River Quaker Cemetery, Lynchburg, Virginia). Thomas and Rachel, both Quakers, married 12 Jan 1729 (Green Spring Quaker Meeting House, Louisa County, Virginia). They had 15 children from 1730 to 1754. Three of Thomas and Rachel's children are detailed in this section: Zachariah (born 1732), Micajah (born 1735), and Agatha (born 1849).

In 1762, Thomas bought 200 acres of land in Bedford County, and moved there with his family on 9 Mar 1767 from Golansville, Caroline County. In Thomas's will, he left 13 slaves as legacies to his spouse and children. After Thomas died, Rachel married William Ballard (1715; 1794) on 25 Aug 1768.

Right: South River Meeting House Graveyard, Lynchburg, Virginia.

Susanna Chiles's parents were **Manoah Chiles** (14 Aug 1706, Kemp House, Jamestown, Virginia; 14 Aug 1760, Caroline County, Virginia) and **Elizabeth Terrell** (1708, Caroline County; Oct 1742, Caroline County, Virginia). Manoah and Elizabeth, both Quakers, were married in 1725 in Caroline, Virginia. They had 7 children from 1726 to 1740. After Elizabeth died, Manoah married Ann Elizabeth Cheadle in Dec 1742. They had 6 children.

~~~

9. Thomas Moorman's parents were **Charles Moorman** (29 Aug 1671, Green Springs, Virginia; 24 May 1757, Green Springs, Virginia) and **Elizabeth Reynolds** (29 Aug 1686, Isle of Wight, Virginia; 11 May 1765, Green Springs, Virginia). Charles and Elizabeth, both Quakers, were married in 1704 in Green Springs, Virginia. They had 6 children from 1705 to 1715. Sometime before 1744, Charles and the family moved to Virginia.

Moormans River, a 14.3-mile tributary in central Virginia that flows through Shenandoah National Park, and is a part of the Chesapeake Bay watershed, was named for Charles Moorman, who in 1735 patented 400 acres of land at the junction of Mechum and Moormans River.

Charles Moorman was a leading Quaker and he and his son Thomas were overseers of the Friends Meeting House on Camp Creek. His will, dated May 9, 1755, was proved in Louisa County, May 24, 1757. In it he mentions his wife and five children: Thomas, Judith, Ann, Achilles, and Charles [son Andrew died in 1755]. (Ackerleys' Our Kin, Bedford County, Virginia, Will Book I, p. 25). The same children are named by his widow, Elizabeth Moorman, in her will dated January 9, 1761, and proved in Louisa County, May 11, 1765.
—*Sketches of the Moon and Barclay Families; including the Harris, Moorman, Johnson, Appling Families*

Will of Charles Moorman, dated May 9, 1755
NOTE: Transcribed by David Kaiser, 01/07/96. The left edge of the will book's page was torn so that 3 to 4 letters of each line were missing. Likely omissions are signified with brackets [ ]; plausible or uncertain omissions are signified with parentheses. Descendant names are capitalized for convenience's sake only.

In the name of God Amen. I, CHARLES MOORMAN, of [Lo]uisa Co being perfect health Sense and memory (attest?) to [Alm]ighty God for the same do acknowledge this to being last will and [testa]ment this ninth day of May in the Year of our Lord One thousand [seven] hundred and fifity five which is as followeth Item I lend unto [my be]loved wife ELIZABETH all my household furniture and Stock of {?} Horses and Mares with four Negores named Toby Jack (Cuffer) ... Dina forher proper use during Widowhood or Life and after her [dea]th these four above named Negores with the Increase and [a]forementioned Goods and Chattels to be Equally dividied between [my] Sons THOMAS CHARLES and ACHELIES MOORMAN. Item I give and [beq]ueath unto my beloved Son CHARLES MOORMAN three hundred (and fifty?} Acres of Land being more or less lying and being on both [s]ides of (Hus?)one Creek the land where on he now Lives to him and [his] heirs and Assigns forever. Item I give and bequeath unto my belo![ved]
Son ACHILIES MOORMAN the Land and Plantation whereon (?..ve Containg) four hundred and twenty Acres More or Less to [to his] heirs & Assigns forever. Item I give & bequeath unto my (?beloved) Sons Thomas CHARLES and ACHILIES MOORMAN four Negores name[d] Harry little Harry Jenny and Nany to be Qualldivided in (?) between all three above named Sons Item I give unto my Daughter JUDITH the wife of John Douglas One Shilling Sterling money. (?Item) I give unto my Daughter ANN the wife of Thomas Martin One Shilling Sterling money and I so appoints (gleave) my three Sons THOMAS CHARLES & ACHILIES MOORMAN with my wfe ELIZABETH Executors & Executris of this my Last Will & Testmant. (?) may not be appraised.
Charles (mark) Moorman (seal)
Signed in Presence of George Taylor, John (mark) Megra, Thomas (mark) Clark
At a court held for Louisa Co the 24th Day of May 1757...

Rachel Clark's parents were **Christopher Thomas Clark, Captain** (14 Aug 1681, Somerton, Virginia; 28 May 1754, Louisa County, Virginia) and **Penelope Johnston** (14 Aug 1684, New Kent, Virginia; 14 Aug 1760, New Kent, Virginia). Christopher and Penelope married in 1709 (Virginia). They had 8 children from 1710 to 1725. Christopher was a captain in the militia, a lawyer, and a merchant. He was justice of the peace in Louisa County in 1742. He is stated to have joined the Quakers in 1742. In 1749, he was appointed overseer of a meeting of Quakers near Sugarloaf Mountain in Albemarle County.

CLARK, CHRISTOPHER, (1681-1754) Quaker. Came from England via Barbados about 1710. Acquired 50,000 acres of land in Hanover, Albermarle and Louisa Cos. Capt. of Hanover Co. militia, High Sheriff, Justice of Louisa Co. Overseer of Friends Meeting near Sugar Loaf Mountain. Law partner of Nicholas Meriwether. Married 1709 Penelope Johnson, daughter of Edward. She died 1754.
—*Early Immigrants to Virginia from the 1500s and 1600s.*

Manoah Chiles's parents were **John Henry Chiles** (4 Apr 1671, Jamestown Colony, Virginia; 27 Feb 1719, Hanover County, Virginia) and **Margaret Littlepage** (1673, New Kent County, Virginia; 1760, Halifax County, Virginia). Henry and Margaret married about 1687. They had 6 children from 1688 to 1707.

Elizabeth Terrell's parents were **Joel Terrell** (22 May 1692, New Kent, Virginia; 1758, Hanover County, Virginia) and **Sarah Elizabeth Oxford** (1698; 1730). Joel and Sarah's parents unknown.

~~~

10. Charles Moorman II's parents were **Thomas Moorman** (1658, Isle of Wight, England; 1713, Green Springs, Virginia) and **Elizabeth Macajah Clark,** later Simpson (1659, New Kent, Virginia; 1700, Green Springs, Virginia). In 1669, Thomas and his parents and siblings sailed from England to the West Indies. In 1670, they sailed to South Carolina. Thomas and Elizabeth married in 1683 in Green Springs, Virginia. They had 6 children from 1684 to 1705.

> Thomas Moorman, son of Mary (Candler) and Zachariah Moorman, became a landed proprietor in South Carolina, having been granted land by the London Company. He later moved to Nansemond County, Virginia, where he was a vestry man in 1679 (Sommerton). In the same year he moved to Green Springs, Louisa Co. He married Elizabeth (presumably Macajah).   —Moorman of Virginia, Mrs. James E. O'Donnell

Elizabeth Reynolds's parents were **Richard Joshua Reynolds** (27 Jul 1641, Isle of Wight, Virginia; 27 Jul 1711, Somerset, Maryland) and **Elizabeth Ann Sharpe, Lady** (1647, Isle of Wight, Virginia; 8 Jul 1754, Isle of Wight, Virginia). Richard and Elizabeth married in 1663 (Virginia). Richard's and Elizabeth's fathers unknown.

Christopher Clark's parents were **Micajah Christopher Clark** (1659, Isle of Wight, England; 28 Mar 1706, Somerton, Virginia) and **Sallie Ann Moorman** (1662, Isle of Wight, England; 1710, Charles City, Virginia). Micajah and Sally married about 1679. They had 9 children from 1679 to 1704. Micajah and Sally Ann (along with their parents) sailed from England to Barbados in 1699. Micajah and Sally Ann went to South Carolina in 1700 and then eventually settled in Virginia.

Penelope Johnston's parents were **Edward Johnston** (21 Apr 1649, Aberdeen, Scotland; 4 May 1704, New Kent, Virginia) and **Elizabeth Sarah Walker** (1655, Virginia; 1725, Virginia). Edward and Elizabeth married in 1677 (Virginia). They had 12 children from 1673 to 1701.

Henry Chiles's parents were **Walter Chiles II, Lt. Colonel** (20 Mar 1631, Somerset, England; 15 Nov 1671, Jamestown, Virginia; buried Chiles Family Cemetery, James City County, Virginia) and **Mary Susannah Page** (25 Jun 1648, London, England; 25 Nov 1671, Jamestown, Virginia). Mary's parents unknown.

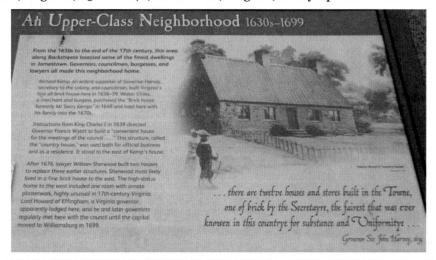

The "Kemp House" (pictured) on Jamestown Island, Virginia was the first brick constructed dwelling in America. It was built in 1638/39 and was sold with its acreage by Governor Sir William Berkeley in 1649 to merchant and Burgess Walter Chiles I for the sum of 26,000 pounds of tobacco. Walter Chiles I died in 1653 resulting in his son, Walter Chiles II, inheriting the structure. Elizabeth Chiles, wife of Walter Chiles I, lived in the house following his death. Her son, Walter Chiles II, and his first wife, Mary Page, also lived in the house for a short time with his mother prior to building a house very close-by on Jamestowne Island.

Margaret Littlepage's parents were **Richard Littlepage** (1639, Oxfordshire, England; 1688, New Kent, Virginia; buried Saint Peter's Episcopal Church Cemetery, Putneys Mill, Virginia) and **Elizabeth Frances Austin** (12 Feb 1650, New Kent, Virginia; 21 Feb 1732, Christ Church, Virginia). Richard and Elizabeth had 2 children from 1673 to 1678. Richard's and Elizabeth's parents unknown.

~~~

11. Thomas Moorman's parents were **Zachariah "Old Zach" Moorman, Captain** (1620, Isle of Wight, England; 1671, Somerton, Nansemond County, Virginia) and **Mary Ann Elizabeth Candler** (1635, Isle of Wight, England; 1670, England). Zachariah and Mary Ann married about 1656. They had 3 children from 1658 to 1662: Thomas, Charles, and Sally Ann (married Micajah Clark). Mary Ann was not with the family when they went to Virginia. Sallie Ann Moorman and Thomas were siblings.

> Zachariah Moorman, the American immigrant of this name, was born in Isle of Wight, England, in 1620. At the age of 19 he joined the British Army and became a Captain in Cromwell's Army in the invasion of Ireland, where he lived for a few years, and, in 1646, married Mary Candler, the daughter of William Candler, a Lieutenant in Cromwell's Army, who had been granted estates in Ireland. Zachariah returned to Isle of Wight, England, but being a sympathizer of Charles II, became an enemy of Cromwell. In the spring of 1669, Zachariah Moorman with his children and son-in-law, Micajah Clark, embared at Southampton, England, in the ship *Glasgow,* and sailed to the Barbadoes Islands in the West Indies. Early in the next springs (1670) they joined the immigrants who sailed for South Carolina, landing near the site of Charleston, where the first permanent colony was being formed. —Moorman of Virginia, Mrs. James E. O'Donnell

Elizabeth Macajah Clark's parents were **Michael Christopher Clark** (1629, Isle of Wight, England; 3 Aug 1678, Barbados, West Indies) and **Margaret Rebecca Yarrett** (6 May 1626, Isle of Wight, England; 22 Dec 1679, Barbados, West Indies). Michael and Rebecca married in 1645. They had 2 children in 1648 and 1659. Elizabeth Clark and Micajah Clark were siblings.

> Michael Clark inherited his father's [Edward Clark] Virginia lands, although he apparently never resided there. In the spring of 1669, he and his family sailed from England, with the Moorman family, to Barbados, where he was a landholder in Christ Church parish. —Find A Grave

Richard Joshua Reynold's mother was **Elizabeth Rivers Matthews** (15 Jul 1615, Canterbury, England; Jan 1658, Isle of Wight, Virginia).

Elizabeth Ann Sharpe's mother was **Ann Harris** (1628, Virginia; 1699, Isle of Wight, Virginia). Father unknown. Ann's parents unknown.

Micajah Christopher Clark's parents were **Michael Christopher Clark** and **Margaret Rebecca Yarrett**. See entries under Elizabeth Macajah Clark. Micajah Clark and Elizabeth Clark were siblings.

Sallie Ann Moorman's parents were **Zachariah "Old Zach" Moorman, Captain,** and **Mary Ann Elizabeth Candler**. See entries under Thomas Moorman. Thomas and Sallie were siblings.

Edward Johnston's parents were **Arthur Johnston, Dr.** (1587, Scotland; 1641, England) and **Barbara Gordon** (1600, Scotland; 1650, Scotland). Arthur's parents unknown.

Elizabeth Sarah Walker's parents were **Alexander Walker, Captain** (1614, Scotland; 1725, Virginia) and **Ann Keith** (1635, New Kent, Virginia; 6 Sep 1702, New Kent, Virginia). Alexander's parents unknown.

Walter Chiles II's parents were **Walter Chiles I** (1608, England; 1653, Virginia) and **Elizabeth Saunders** (1602, England; 1672, Virginia). Walter and Elizabeth were married about 1627.

~~~

12. Captain Zachariah "Old Zach" Moorman's parents were **Thomas Moorman, "Man of the Moor"** (1593, Isle of Wight, England; 1640, Isle of Wight, England) and **Ida Brading** (1593, Hampshire, England; 1620, Isle of Wight, England). Thomas and Ida married in 1620.

> In 1624 Thomas Moorman was give shares in the Virginia Land Company of London, along with John Clarke, the Navigator o the *Bona Nova,* and the *Mayflower* of 1620. Thomas Moorman came on the *Bona Nova* in 1619 as an Officer of the British Army. In 1625 Thomas Moorman "Yeoman" won a suit over tithes of Bronchurch which he had refused to pay. When he was in Virginia (Jamestown) he received word that his wife had born a son, 1620, Zachariah Moorman. —*The Moorman Family,* Patricia Stanely, July 1995.

Mary Ann Elizabeth Candler's parents were **William Astor Candler, Lt. Colonel** (25 Sep 1608, Suffolk, England; 1680, Kilkenny, Ireland) and **Elizabeth Anne Anthony** (1612, Hampshire, England; 1654, Kilkenny, Ireland). William and Elizabeth married in 1632.

Michael Christopher Clark's parents were **Thomas Edward Clark** (1602, Isle of Wight, England; 17 Sep 1661, Cambridgeshire, England) and **Diana Hayward** (11 Oct 1611, Suffolk, England; 1629, Isle of Wight, England). Diana's parents unknown.

> Edward Clark was listed as an ancient planter of Virginia, 1614-16, and again in Feb 1623. In 1624, he was awarded 200 acres by the Virginia Company, as a result of his late father's service. While the identity of his wife is not known, he evidently returned to England, resettling at his birthplace.   —Find A Grave

Margaret Rebecca Yarrett's parents were **William Yarrett, Sir** (Oct 1600, Isle of Wight, England; 9 Mar 1679, Isle of Wight, Virginia) and **Margaret Wiggs** (1611, Virginia; 1677, Virginia). William and Margaret married in 1620. They had 6 children from 1622 to 1656. Margaret's parents unknown.

Elizabeth Rivers Matthews's parents were **Anthony Matthews** (1582, England; 1640, Isle of Wight, Virginia) and **Elizabeth Boddie** (1582, London, England; 1657, Bertie, North Carolina). Anthony and Elizabeth married in 1610. Anthony's and Elizabeth's parents unknown.

Barbara Gordon's parents were **John Gordon, Sir** (1570, Aberdeenshire, Scotland; 1622, Scotland) and **Margaret Udny** (1581, Scotland; Callen Castle, Ireland). John's parents unknown.

Alexander Walker's parents were **Samuel Thomas Walker, Rev.** (6 Apr 1570 (Nottinghamshire, England; 22 Mar 1622, New Kent, Virginia) and **Elizabeth Amery Sherrill** (1585 (Nottinghamshire, England; 17 May 162, South Carolina). Samuel's and Elizabeth's parents unknown.

Ann Keith's parents were **William Keith, 6th Earl of Marischal** (1585, Scotland; 1635, Dunnottar Castle, Scotland) and **Mary Margaret Erskine, Lady** (1593, Scotland; 1664, Dunnottar Castle, Scotland). William and Mary married in 1609 (Dunnottar Castle, Scotland). They had 8 children from 1614 to 1635. William's and Mary's parents unknown.

Left: Dunnotar Castle, Scotland. Right: Mary, Countess Marischal, and son John, portrait by George Jamesone.

Dunnotar Castle is a ruined fortress located upon a rocky headland on the northeastern coast of Scotland, about 2 miles south of Stonehaven. The surviving buildings are largely of the 15th and 16th centuries, but the site is believed to have been fortified in the Early Middle Ages (5th century). The castle was sold in 1717 and the title of Earl Marischal ended. In 1925, the castle was saved from ruin and is now a tourist destination.

Walter Chiles Sr.'s parents were **Walter Chiles** (1572, Wrighton, England; 1653, Jamestown, Virginia) and **Elizabeth Maury** (1580, England; 1672, Virginia). Walter and Elizabeth married in 1597 (England). Elizabeth's parents unknown.

Elizabeth Saunders's parents were **John Sanders** (1592-1619) and **Alice Coles** (1591-1636). John's and Alice's parents unknown.

~~~

13. Thomas Moorman's parents were **Thomas Moorman Sr.** (1559, Isle of Wight, England; 1593, Isle of Wight, England) and **Elizabeth (Clerke) Clark** (1562, Kent, England; 1617, Isle of Wight, England). Thomas and Elizabeth married in 1590. Thomas and Elizabeth's parents unknown.

Ida Brading's parents were **Richard Brading** (1572, Isle of Wight, England; 1634, Isle of Wight, England) and **Joane Fowle** (6 May 1568, Kent, England; ~1631, Isle of Wight, England).

William Candler's parents were **William Astor Candler** (21 Jun 1582, Suffolk, England; 18 Dec 1612, Suffolk, England) and **Hannah Fiske** (1582, Suffolk, England; 25 Nov 1616, Suffolk, England). William and Hannah married on 4 May 1603. They had 5 children from 1603 to 1611.

> married.   5. Hannah, married, May 4, 1603, William Candler; he was schoolmaster at Tofford; their son, Rev. Matthias Candler, was author of the celebrated Candler Manuscript on file in the British Museum; other children were John and Mary Candler.   6. Hester,
>
> —*Genealogical and Family History of Western New York*

Elizabeth Anne Anthony's parents were **John Anthony, Dr.** (1585, London, England; 1655, London, England) and **Mary Wigg** (1589, London, England; 18 Aug 1640, London, England). John and Mary married in 1605. They had 5 children from 1607 to after 1613. Mary's parents unknown.

> John Anthony was *b.* in London, 1585. He graduated at Pembroke College in 1613, and was graduated as a physician six years later, in 1619. He was admitted Licentiate of the College of Physicians in 1625. He served during the Civil War on the Parliamentary side as surgeon to Colonel Sandys. He was the author of a devotional work called "The Comfort of the Soul." In the British Museum is a small note-book bound with the Coat of Arms of Charles I, which belonged to John Anthony. He *m.* in London.
>
> —*Colonial Families of the United States, 1607–1775*

> ANTHONY (JOHN), son of above [Dr. Francis Anthony], to whose practice he succeeded, made a handsome living by the sale of his father's medicine called Aurum potabile [liqueur made from brandy, colored with saffron, flavored with oranges, orange zest, and herbs, with particles of gold suspended in it]. He was also author of "Lucas redivivus, or The gospel physician, prescribing (by way of meditation) divine physic to prevent diseases not yet entered upon the soul, and to cure those maladies which have already seized upon the spirit," 1656, 4to. He died April 28, 1655, aged 70, as appears by the monument erected for his father and himself in the church of St. Bartholomew the Great in London.
>
> —*Chalmers General Biographical Dictionary*

Thomas Edward Clark's parents were **John Clarke** (1575, England; 1623, Jamestown, Virginia) and **Mary Morton Kerridge** (1577, England; 1605, England). John's and Mary's parents unknown.

> John was the Master's Mate and pilot of the *Mayflower* and accompanied the Pilgrims on many of the exploring parties, piloting the shallop [sailboat for coastal navigation]. Clark's Island in Duxbury Bay [Plymouth, Massachusetts] is named after him, because he miraculously brought the shallop ashore during a strong storm on one of these expeditions. John was given two shares in the Virginia Company for his service. He sailed to Virginia on 10 April 1623 in Daniel Gookin's ship, the *Providence,* and died shortly after he arrived.   —Ancestry.com entry

> John Clark first went to Jamestown, Virginia, in March 1610 as a ship's pilot. There, at Point Comfort, he was captured by the Spanish in June 1611. He was taken captive at Havana, Cuba, where he was interrogated, and then sent to Seville, Spain, and then on to Madrid in 1613. He was held as a prisoner until he was ransomed by King James I in exchange for a Spanish prisoner held by the English in 1616. He immediately went back to his occupation as a ship's pilot, and took a shipment of cattle to Jamestown, Virginia, in 1619 under sometime pirate Thomas Jones. In 1620, he was hired to be the master's mate and pilot of the *Mayflower,* on its intended voyage to Northern Virginia. While the Pilgrims were exploring Cape Cod and Plymouth Harbor, the shallop was caught in a storm and Clark brought them safely ashore at an Island, which it to this day known as Clark's Island. After returning, John Clark decided to settle in Virginia himself. He went to Jamestown in 1623 on the

ship *Providence,* with the intention of settling there, but died not too long after his arrival. John was a Quaker and he did not sign The Mayflower Compact. —Ancestry.com entry

William Yarrett's parents were **Adam Yarrett** (1570, Isle of Wight, England; 14 Oct 1666, Isle of Wight, England) and **Rachel Rhodes** (1590, Isle of Wight, England; 1677, Isle of Wight, England). Adam and Rachel married in 1608. Adam's and Rachel's parents unknown.

Margaret Udny's parents were **William Udny, Sir** (1550, Scotland; 1597, Scotland) and **Matilda Gordon, Lady** (1555, Scotland; 1581, Scotland). William and Matilda's parents unknown.

Walter Chiles's parents were **William Childe** (1529, Wrighton, England; 1616, Wrighton, England) and **Margaret Payne** (1537, England; 1625, Wrighton, England). William and Margaret married 1565 (England). William's and Margaret's parents unknown.

~~~

14. Richard Brading's parents were **Richard Brading** (1544, Isle of Wight, England; Aug 1582, Isle of Wight, England) and **Jone Dagewell** (30 Aug 1546, Isle of Wight, England; 1583, Isle of Wight, England). Jone's mother unknown.

Joane Fowle's parents were **Thomas Fowle** (1540, Kent, England; 25 Aug 1592, Kent, England) and **Joane Pope** (1545, England; 1570, England). Thomas's and Joane's parents unknown.

William Astor Candler's parents were **Ralph Candler** (1562, Suffolk, England; 1582, Essex, England) and **Ann Thoroughgood** (19 Nov 1569, Hertfordshire, England; 6 Dec 1630, Hertfordshire, England). Ralph and Ann married in 1582. Ralph's and Ann's parents unknown.

Hannah Fiske's parents were **William Fiske** (1550, Suffolk, England; 17 May 1623, Norfolk, England) and **Elizabeth** (1553, Norfolk, England; 17 May 1620, Norfolk, England). William's and Elizabeth's parents unknown.

John Anthony's parents were **Francis Anthony, Dr.** (16 Apr 1550, London, England; 6 May 1623, London England) and **Susan "Alice" Elsa Howe, Lady** (1554, England; 26 May 1623, England). Francis and Susan married in 1582. They had 4 children from 1585 to 1597.

Francis Anthony was a noted English apothecary and physician, imprisoned twice for practicing without a license. He made a considerable fortune from a secret remedy he developed called aurum potabile. He arrived in London in 1598 and commenced medical practice without a proper license; after six months, he was called before the president and censors of the Royal College of Physicians (a.d. 1600), and banned from practicing, after being examined in medicine and found inexpert. However he disregarded the injunction, and was subsequently fined five pounds and committed to prison; he was released by a warrant of the Lord Chief Justice. The college, however, objected and he was returned to prison. Later, Anthony was again prosecuted for the same offense of unlicensed practice and ordered to pay a heavy fine; he refused and was jailed for eight months, being released at the petition of his wife, and on the ground of poverty, in 1602. He continued to practise in defiance of the college, and further proceedings were threatened, but not carried out, probably because Anthony had powerful friends at court. His practice consisted chiefly, if not entirely, in the prescription and sale of a secret remedy called *aurum potabile*, from which he made a considerable fortune. —Wikipedia

Memorial for Francis Anthony at St. Bartholomew in London.

~~~

15. Richard Brading's parents were **John Brading** (1510, Isle of Wight, England; 1571, Isle of Wight, England) and **Elizabeth Coleman** (1510, Isle of Wight, England; Sep 1598, Whitewell, England). John's and Elizabeth's parents unknown.

Jone Dagewell's father was **John Ralph Dagwell** (1510, Isle of Wight, England; 26 Sep 1570, Isle of Wight, England). John's parents unknown.

Francis Anthony's parents were **Derrick Francis Anthony, Lord** (1525, London, England; 1558, London, England) and **Judith Roby** (1527, London, England; 1570, London, England). Derrick was a goldsmith and held a position in the jewel office of Queen Elizabeth. Derrick and Judith married in 1549. They had 4 children from 1550 to 1557. Derrick's and Judith's parents unknown.

Susan "Alice" Howe's parents were **Thomas Howe** (1523, Somerset, England; 1574, Somerset, England) and **Elizabeth Gerther** (1526, London, England; 1558, London, England). Thomas's and Elizabeth's parents unknown.

~~~

Elizabeth "Betty" Johnson Moorman

Born 24 Oct 1768, Cedar Creek, Hanover County, Virginia; died 6 Sep 1827 at age 58, Fall Creek, Highland, Ohio; unknown burial location. Betty was a Quaker. At the age of 20, Betty married Charles Moorman on 2 Dec 1788 in Amelia County, Virginia. Betty and Charles shared grandparents (Thomas and Rachel Moorman). They had 9 children from 1792 to 1811. Her son William Moorman was born in 1792 when Betty was 24. Her last child was born in 1811 when Betty was 43.

Quaker records indicated that on 28 Feb 1789, Betty was "disowned" from the Quaker faith for marrying a man too near of kin. On 12 May 1791, she condemned the marriage that was "contrary to the discipline" and requested reinstatement. On 14 Jan 1791, Betty condemned the misconduct and was reinstated. On 25 Feb 1792, Betty transferred to the South River group in Virginia.

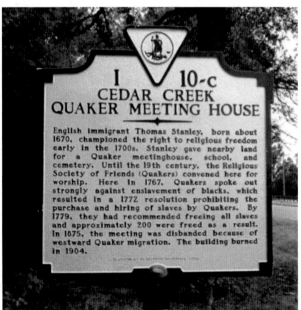

Betty Johnson Moorman's Ancestors beyond Sixth Generation

7. Betty Johnson's parents were **William Johnson Sr.** (22 Aug 1739, Cedar Creek, Virginia; 14 Aug 1824, Leesburg, Highland County, Ohio) and **Agatha Moorman** (18 Sep 1749, Cedar Creek, Virginia; 19 May 1823, Fairfield, Highland County, Ohio). William and Agatha, both Quakers, married on 10 Dec 1763. They had 13 children from 1766 to 1791. William's parents unknown.

William and Agatha were members of the Cedar Creek Quakers. On 9 May 1789, they and their children transferred to the South River group in Campbell County, Virginia. Two of Agatha's siblings are detailed in this section: Zachariah (born 1732) and Micajah (born 1735).

~~~

8. Agatha Moorman's parents were **Thomas Moorman** (14 Sep 1705, Green Springs, Virginia; 10 Nov 1767, Lynchburg, Virginia) and **Rachel Clark,** later Ballard (14 Jun 1714, New Kent, Virginia; 10 Jun 1792, Bedford, Virginia).

Follow these ancestors under Charles Moorman to the 15th generation.

~~~

Charles and Betty Moorman Summary

Charles Moorman (21) and Elizabeth "Betty" Johnson (20), both Quakers, married in 1788 (Amelia County, Virginia). They had 9 children in 19 years. In 1806, Charles, Betty, and their 6 children transferred from the South River Monthly Meeting (MM), Virginia, to the Miami MM, Ohio.

In the 1800s, many Quakers left Virginia to travel to Ohio because of slavery. Many thought they couldn't live in a community where slavery was an economic cornerstone. Others migrated because of the Revolutionary War. If a Quaker member joined the Army, he was disowned by the Quakers. After the war, they were often reinstated to the faith. These soldiers received land from the government for services rendered, and often the land was in Ohio.

1. **William** (8/10 Mar 1792, Virginia; 8 Jan 1870, Iowa) married Kitty Johnson (1798; 1874) on 29 Jan 1817 (Fairfield, Ohio). They had 10 children. See details in Paternal Fifth Generation.

2. **Nancy Paxson** (20 Jul 1796, Virginia; after 1821, Ohio) married John Overman (1797; 1845) on 31 Jan 1816 (Highland County, Ohio). They had 1 child: *Elizabeth* (1821; 1902).

3. **Fanny Herndon** (10 Apr 1798, Virginia; 1826?) married William Davis (1778; ?) on 14 Feb 1816 (Highland County, Ohio). William Davis married Tena Ferver on 13 Jun 1826 (Fairfield, Ohio).

4. **Robert Alexander** (15 Feb 1801, Virginia; 11 Aug 1856, Iowa) married Mary Ann Adair (1806; 1864) on 12 Aug 1828 (Highland County, Ohio). They had 5 children: *Charles J. "C. J."* (1829; after 1885) a tin maker/tinner, Civil War Union private in Iowa, Company C, 45th Infantry (May 1864–Sep 1864); *John Overman* (1832; 1880); *William T.* (1834; 1868) Civil War veteran; *Martha Ann* (1837; 1872); *Perry A.* (1847; 1852) died age 5. In the **1850 US Census,** Robert was listed as a shoemaker, son John was a sawyer, and son William was a carder. In the **1855 Iowa Census,** son John was listed as an engineer, son William was listed as a mill sawyer. Martha A. Fletcher (17) and Rosetta Fletcher (infant) were also living in the home with Robert and Mary. Robert is buried in White Cemetery, Oskaloosa, Iowa.

In William T. Moorman's will, dated 20 Jun 1868, he bequeathed 80 acres in Keokuk, Iowa, with improvements and homestead to his brother John O. Moorman; he gave an adjoining 80 acres to his brother Charles J. Moorman. He gave $500 to his sister Martha A. Moore (payable $100 per year). In addition, "I will and bequeath to Miss Elizabeth Brooks one gold watch of the value of one hundred and fifty dollars to be purchased by my executor within twelve months after my decease." Unable to determine who Miss Brooks was.

5. **Elizabeth "Betsy"** (1803, Virginia; 1825) died age 22.

6. **Agatha** (1806, Virginia; Mar 1866) married Charles M. Johnson (1802; 1870) on 13 Nov 1823 (Highland County, Ohio). They had 9 children: *William S.* (1825; before 1880); *Havilah B.* (1826; 1881) a Civil War Union veteran, private, Illinois Company F, 112th Infantry (1862–1864); *Horace Asbury* (1830; 1866); *Lucy Ann* (1837; 1858); *John T.* (1841; after 1870) a peddler; *Charles S.* (1845; 1863) a waiter, served in US Civil War, private, Company B, 33rd Illinois Infantry (1861–1863), died of disease and "Intermit. Fever" at G. H. Ironton, Missouri; *Mary E.* (1848; 1848); *Henry T.* (after 1824; 1845); *George* (after 1824; 1850). In the **1850 US Census,** Charles was listed as a carpenter, his son Havilah was listed as a painter; his son Horace was listed as a laborer. In the **1860 US Census,** Charles's sons John and Charles were listed as day laborers.

7. **Susan** (1807, Ohio; after 1880) married William Ballard (1805; 1873) a lawyer, nurseryman, painter, served in the Civil War (Union) private, Iowa, Company E, 37th Infantry (1862–1863), discharged with disability. They had 7 children. *Sarah E.* (1831; after 1850); *Achilles William* (1833; 1898) painter; *Thomas M.* (1835; 1918) an engineer, gunsmith; *William Henry* (1839; after 1860) an engineer; *Caroline A.* (1842; after 1860) seamstress; *Madison T.* (1844; after 1880), laborer, fanning, laborer; *Uriah* (1846; 1916), day laborer, clerking. Susan had rheumatism when she was 72.

> Civil War Veteran, Co E 37th Iowa Infantry, "The Greybeard Regiment" Ballard, William. Age 56. Residence Oskaloosa, Iowa, nativity Virginia. Enlisted Sept. 4, 1862. Mustered Dec. 15, 1862. Discharged for disability April 28, 1863, St. Louis, Mo. The Greybeard Regiment has a unique place in history. It was

the only regiment made up of men over the enlistment or draft age which at that time was 45. All were volunteers...some as old as 80 years. Its purpose was to guard prisons and arsenals to free young men for battle however it did see action when guarding supply trains and defending Memphis, TN during a surprise attack from the infamous cavalry of Nathan Bedford Forrest.   —Find A Grave

8. **Thomas** (7 Sep 1809, Ohio; 26 Mar 1889, Iowa) a farmer, married (1) Margaret Canady (1814; 1854) on 16 Apr 1833 (Highland County, Ohio). They had 9 children: ***Anna Elizabeth*** (1834; 1919); ***Elizabeth "Eliza" Ellen*** (1835; 1870) died at home of typhoid fever; ***Amanda Jane*** (1837; 1895); ***Charles Walter*** (1838; 1918) served in the US Civil War, Union, 4th sergeant promoted to 3rd sergeant, Iowa, Company F, 3rd Cavalry (1861–1862); ***Albert Matthew*** (1841; 1847) died age 6; ***Martha Maria*** (1844; 1923); ***William Thomas*** (1846; 1935) served in the US Civil War, private, Company I, 45th Infantry; died of a "cerebral emboli" at age 87; ***Lewis Clark*** (1849; 1850) died 11 months; ***Sarah Alice*** (1850; 1900). After Margaret died in 1854, Thomas married (2) Leah Beauchamp Brooks Robinson (1826; 1910) on 19 Apr 1859 (Fairfield, Iowa). Eva had 5 children from a previous marriage. In the **1860 US Census,** there were 9 children living in the home with Thomas and Leah in Fairfield, Iowa. Thomas and Leah had 1 child: ***Eva C.*** (1863; 1885). In the **1880 US Census,** Thomas and Leah were at home with daughter Eva (16), niece Marcella Moorman (20), and grandson Claud Combes (6).

9. **Charles** (1811, Ohio; 1830) died age 19.

<p style="text-align:center">~~~</p>

Left: Charles and Betty's son Robert Alexander Moorman, White Cemetery, Oskaloosa, Iowa, died age 55.
Middle and right: Charles and Betty's grandson John Overman Moorman, White Cemetery, Oskaloosa, Iowa, died age 47.

Left: Charles and Betty's grandson William T. Moorman, White Cemetery, Oskaloosa, Iowa, died age 34.
Middle: Charles and Betty's son Thomas Moorman, Moorman Cemetery, Fairfield, Iowa, died age 79.
Right: Charles and Betty's grandson Thomas M. Ballard, Masonic IOOF Cemetery, Montezuma, Iowa, died age 81.

Rev. Thomas W. Grafton
Pastor
Third Christian Church
Broadway & 17th St.
2211 Broadway

Charles and Betty's grandson Thomas W. Grafton (1857; 1940).

Minister of the Disciples of Christ Church. The son of Parker Baker Grafton and Elizabeth Moorman Grafton of Iowa, Rev. Thomas Grafton was the pastor of the Third Christian Church of Indianapolis for 15 years, from 1912 to 1927. An 1880 graduate of Butler College, he served at other churches in Indiana, Illinois, Michigan and Missouri, and he later taught Religion at Butler University, his old alma mater. He came to California after retiring from active ministry in 1931. He wrote extensively for evangelical journals, and was the author of a book on the life of Alexander Campbell, an early leader of the Disciples of Christ. Husband of Anna J. (Johnson) Grafton, and father of Rev. Warren Grafton and Allena Grafton.
     —Find A Grave

Left: Charles and Betty's granddaughter Eliza Ellen Moorman Junkin, Moorman Cemetery, Fairfield, Iowa, died age 35.
Right: Charles and Betty's granddaughter Amanda Jane Wilkins Atlantic Cemetery, Atlantic, Iowa, died age 58.

Charles and Betty's grandson Charles W. Moorman

WPA Records—Co. F. 3rd IA. Cav.; s/o Thos. & Margaret Canady Mooreman; Chr. Maggie, Hazel Moorman Oliver. Co.F. Third Iowa Cavalry—Moorman, Charles W. Age 23. Residence Fairfield, nativity Ohio. Enlisted Aug. 26, 1861, as Fourth Sergeant. Mustered Aug. 30, 1861. Promoted Third Sergeant Oct. 8, 1861. Discharged Feb. 8, 1862.   —Find A Grave

Left: Charles and Betty's grandson Albert Matthew Moorman, Moorman Cemetery, Fairfield, Iowa, died age 6.
Right: Charles and Betty's granddaughter Martha Moorman, Ottumwa Cemetery, Ottumwa, Iowa, died age 78.

Charles and Betty's granddaughter Martha Maria Moorman and her spouse Benjamin Webster Searle, MD.

Charles and Betty's grandson William Thomas Moorman, Evergreen Cemetery, Fairfield, Iowa, died age 87.

W.T. MOORMAN DIES IN CITY

Civil War Veteran is Called At the Home of His Daughter

William T. Moorman, civil war veteran who was born December 7, 1847 in Jefferson county, died at the home of his daughter, Mrs. Hattie Davis, 202 North Sixth street, about 9:30 p.m. yesterday. He is survived by two children, Mrs. Davis at whose hoe he died, and Everett (sic. Ernest) Moorman, of Greely, Colo. His wife preceded him in death December 26, 1902. He had lived in Fairfield for 45 years, and had made his home with his daughter the last four years. He had been seriously ill for about two weeks. Mr. Moorman was a private in Company I, 45th Infantry and served in the civil war. The body was taken to the Hoskins funeral home in this city. Funeral services for William T. Moorman, civil war veteran, who died here Wednesday, will be held at the Methodist church Sunday at 2:30 p.m. in charge of Dr. U. S. Smith. The body will be taken from the Hoskins funeral home to the home of his daughter, Mrs. Hattie Davis where he died, on Sunday morning; it will later be removed to the church at 1:30 p.m. The Daughters of Veterans service will be held at the church. Burial will be in Evergreen cemetery.

—Fairfield Daily Ledger, 7 Mar 1935

**Left: Charles and Betty's grandson Lewis Clark Moorman, Moorman Cemetery, Fairfield, Iowa, died age 11 months.
Middle: Charles and Betty's granddaughter Alice M. Campbell, Florence Cemetery, Florence, Alabama, died age 49.
Right: Charles and Betty's granddaughter Eva C. Moorman Ganier, Moorman Cemetery, Fairfield, Iowa, died age 21.**

Mrs. W. M. Campbell's Death.

On Tuesday morning last, in the early hours of the day, Mrs. Alice M. Campbell, wife of our townsman, Mr. W. M. Campbell, passed peacefully away, after an acute illness of eight weeks. Thus has passed from our midst one of our most popular and beloved ladies, one who was held in the highest esteem for her many noble traits of character. Mrs. Campbell was born in Fairfield, Iowa, fifty years ago. She came with her family to Florence over twelve years ago, and at once formed many social ties, and was always ready to perform her part in the religious and social life of our city. She had been in delicate health for a long time, but for eight weeks past her condition has been critical, and her friends felt that her span of life was nearly ended. All that medical skill and faithful attention could accomplish was affectionately rendered, but without avail, and at 6 o'clock in the morning the silver cord was broken and the pure spirit took its flight to the eternal home. On Wednesday morning, after religious services in the Presbyterian church, conducted by the pastor, Rev. Harris E. Kirk, the body was consigned to its last resting place in our city cemetery, where the grave was literally covered with flowers contributed by many friends. Mrs. Campbell is survived by her husband and one son, to whom the heartfelt sympathies of our people are extended in this hour of their sore bereavement.   —Find A Grave

~~~

William Moorman is the Moorman family ancestor. See details in the Paternal Fifth Generation.

~~~

Joseph Ellison Johnson

Born 1 Oct 1763, Cedar Creek, Virginia; died 11 Feb 1844 at age 81, Jamestown, Ohio. Buried Seneca Graveyard, Jamestown, Ohio. He was a member of the Quaker Richmond and Cedar Creek Monthly Meetings. Joseph married Agatha Agnes Moorman 19 Mar 1785, Lynchburg, Virginia. They had 10 children from 1786 to 1807.

Joseph Ellison Johnson's Ancestors beyond Sixth Generation

7. Joseph Ellison Johnson's parents were **John Johnson III** (20 May 1734, Amelia, Virginia; 31 Aug 1816, Lynchburg, Virginia; buried South River Meeting House Graveyard, Lynchburg, Virginia) and **Lydia Watkins** (20 May 1734, Hanover County, Virginia; 1779, Guilford, North Carolina). John and Lydia married 13 Jul 1754 (Hanover, Virginia). They had 9 children from 1755 to 1779. Lydia's parents unknown.

~~~

8. John Johnson III's parents were **John Johnson II** (22 Nov 1702, New Kent, Virginia; 29 Jun 1783, Amelia, Virginia) and **Elizabeth Ellison** (22 Nov 1702, New Kent, Virginia; 29 Jun 1783, Amelia, Virginia). John and Elizabeth married in 1725. Elizabeth's parents unknown.

~~~

9. John Johnson II's parents were **John Johnson** (1677, Scotland; 6 Nov 1714, New Kent, Virginia) and **Lucretia Elizabeth Massie** (1677, New Kent, Virginia; 23 Nov 1711, New Kent, Virginia). John's and Elizabeth's parents unknown.

~~~

Agatha Agnes Moorman Johnson

Born 13 May 1767, Caroline County, Virginia; died 26 Jul 1808 at age 41, Lynchburg, Virginia. Buried South River Meeting House Graveyard, Lynchburg, Virginia. She was a member of the Quaker South River Monthly Meeting in Virginia. Agatha married Joseph Ellison Johnson 19 Mar 1785, Lynchburg, Virginia. They had 10 children from 1786 to 1807.

Agatha Agnes Moorman.

Agatha Agnes Moorman Johnson's Ancestors beyond Sixth Generation

7. Agatha Agnes Moorman's parents were **Zachariah William Moorman** (2 Feb 1732, Hanover County, Virginia; 1789, Campbell County, Virginia; buried Liberty University—Moorman Cemetery, Lynchburg, Virginia) and **Elizabeth Ann "Betty" Terrell** (7 Sep 1738, Caroline County, Virginia; 26 Jul 1773, Beford County, Virginia; buried Liberty University—Moorman Cemetery, Lynchburg, Virginia). Zachariah and Betty married in 1755. They had 5 children from 1758 to 1772. Betty's parents unknown.

8. Zachariah William Moorman's parents were **Thomas Moorman** (1705-1767) and **Rachel Clark Moorman,** later Ballard (1714-1792). Two of Zachariah's siblings are detailed in this section: Micajah (born 1735) and Agatha (born 1849).

Follow these ancestors under Charles Moorman to the 15th generation.

Elizabeth Ann "Betty" Terrell's parents were **Henry Terrell** (1 Jan 1704, Hanover, Virginia; Apr 1760, Caroline County, Virginia) and **Ann Elizabeth Chiles** (1709, Hanover, Virginia; 3 Apr 1744, Caroline County, Virginia). Henry and Ann married in 1734 (Hanover, Virginia). Henry and Ann's parents unknown.

~~~

Joseph and Agatha Johnson Summary

Joseph Ellison Johnson (21) and Agatha Agnes Moorman (17) married on 19 Mar 1785 (Lynchburg, Virginia). They had 9 children in 19 years.

1. Simeon O. (20 Jun 1786, Virginia; 17 Sep 1849, Iowa) married (1) Delilah Carroll (~1780; 1806) on 15 Sep 1804 (Virginia). They had 1 child: ***Alfred Carroll*** (1806; 1824) died age 17. Simeon was a Quaker South River Monthly Meeting member in Virginia. Delilah was not a Quaker, so Simeon "married contrary to discipline." In 1809, Simeon was "granted certificate to" transfer to Fairfield Monthly Meeting, Ohio.

Simeon married (2) Nancy Johnson (1791; 1833) in 1812. They had 8 children: ***Delilah Albertina*** (1813; 1891) married Dr. Jacob Smith Dalbey (1812; 1866) a physician and Methodist minister, on 22 Aug 1833 (Ohio). They had 13 children: Simeon Johnson (1835; 1919), Joseph Walter (1838; 1917), Milo Alonzo (1839; 1897), Nancy A. (1842; 1854), Arzilla (1844; 1880), Joel Leander (1846; 1917), Susan E. (1848; 1851), Julia A. (1849; 1862), Mary Margaret "Maggie" (1853; 1919), Frances Lydia (1854; 1910), Alice "Allie" C. (1856; 1916), Louisa (1860-1866; ?), unknown girl (1860-1866; ?). ***Emmaline Moriah*** (1814; 1831) died age 16. ***Caroline Agnys*** (1816; 1838) died age 21. ***Charlotte Watkins*** (1819; 1821) died age 1. ***Arzelia*** (1821; 1872) married Andrew Jackson Wilson (1815; 1911). They had 4 children: William Burnworth (1836; 1910), Alfred Selkirk (1847; 1870), Mattie A. (1849; 1937), Sarah M. (1851; 1938). ***Dulys Erskine*** (1823; 1824) died age 1. ***Martha A. Melvina*** (1826; 1846) married Theophilus T. Watkins (1823; 1881) married in 1845 (Ohio). Theophilus served in the Civil War, 13th Regiment of Iowa Volunteers and was wounded at Shiloh. Melvina died age 20, three weeks after giving birth to Simeon L. (1846; 1925). ***Eliza Ann*** (1831; 1896) married John Lewis Bryan (1821; 1911) in 1849 (Iowa). They had 10 children: Milton (1850; 1879), Laura A. (1850; 1876), Leroy Allen (1852; 1923), Mary Alice (1856; 1946), Ida May (1858; 1934), Oscar S. (1862; 1897), Minnie Rose (1864; 1936), Hellen Geneva "Jennie" (1868; 1948), Frank (1870; after 1885), Irene (1879; after 1880).

Simeon married (3) Rachel Cruzen (1804; 1845) on 21 Nov 1833 (Ohio). They had 6 children: ***Rachel Ellen*** (1835; 1878) never married. ***James Madison*** (1838; 1847) died age 9. ***Simeon Oscar*** (1838; 1912) married Martha Horner (1838; 1915) in 1867 (Iowa). They had 6 children: Arthur Ernest (1868; 1915), Bessie B. (1870; 1886), Mary Elizabeth (1872; 1916), William L. (1873; 1909), Chesley Friend "Ted" (1875; 1953), John Wesley (1877; 1951), World War 1 veteran. Simeon was in the US Civil War Mahaska County, Iowa, 8th Infantry, Company H. The family migrated to Oregon about 1873. ***Isabella A. "Belle"*** (1839; 1912) married (1) John E. Watkins (1835; 1865). They had 2 children: Ida Iowa (1857; 1943), Laura A. Watkins (1863; 1912). John was in the US Civil War, Union, private, Iowa, Company B, 40th Infantry (1862–1865). Died of "disease." Belle married (2) John S. Latchem (1825; 1878) in 1868. He had 1 child from his first marriage: Isabelle M. (1854; 1919). John's first spouse died in 1866. Belle and John had 2 children: Margaret E. "Maggie" (1868; 1954), Nellie E. (1870; 1878) died age 8. Belle married (3) Francis "Frank" A. Durham (1859; 1935) in 1880 (Iowa). They had 2 children: Simeon Elwood (1881; 1946), John C. (1882; 1964). ***Helen Elizabeth*** (1841; 1923) married Abraham W. Bailey (1828; 1910). They had 1 child: Elmer E. (1861; 1925). ***William Laban*** (1843; 1918) married Abigail Coffin (1844; 1910). They had 6 children: Simeon Andrew (1863; 1864), Lillie Mae (1865; 1952), Nellie E. (1866; 1924), Jessie Coffin (1872; 1932), Riley Russel (1874; ?), Clyde Earl (1883; 1929).

Simeon married (4) Eliza Jordan (1806; 1868) in 1845. Simeon and Eliza and the family migrated to Iowa in October 1847.

2. Joseph (10 Feb 1788, Virginia; 5 Jul 1847, Illinois) married Hannah Adair (1794; 1856). They had 1 child: ***Madison Y.*** (1817; 1890). Joseph was a Quaker South River Monthly Meeting member in Virginia.

3. Virginia Elizabeth "Betsy" (22 Jan 1790, Virginia; 4 May 1863, Virginia) married John Hope Moorman (1783; after 1860) on 12 Jul 1806. They had 4 children: ***Virginia*** (1830; after 1850), ***Mousesse*** (1832; after 1850), ***Betsy M.*** (1837; after 1850), ***Elizabeth A.*** (1839; after 1860) Betsy and John were Quaker South River Monthly Meeting members in Virginia.

4. John (24 Jul 1793, Virginia; 12 Jul 1876) married Frances Graves (?; ?). John was a Quaker South River Monthly Meeting member in Virginia.

5. Mary "Polly" (16 Dec 1795, Virginia; ?). Polly was a Quaker South River Monthly Meeting member in Virginia.

6. Katherine "Kitty" Winston (15 Mar 1798, Virginia; 6 Jul 1874, Iowa) married William Moorman (1792; 1870) on 29 Jan 1817 (Ohio). They had 10 children. See details in Paternal Fifth Generation. Kitty and William were Quaker South River Monthly Meeting (MM) members in Virginia and later Pleasant Plain MM in Iowa.

7. Elvira "Elvey/Elvy" (29 Aug 1800, Virginia; ?, Ohio). Elvy was a Quaker South River Monthly Meeting member in Virginia.

8. Watkins (23 Jan 1803, Virginia; 1867, Ohio) married (1) Elizabeth Moorman (1803; 1824) on 30 Oct 1822 (Ohio). No children. Watkins married (2) Mary Ann Haller (1807; 1897) on 9 Mar 1827 (Virginia). They had 5 children: ***Marshall Henry*** (1828; 1898). ***William H.*** (1828; before 1830). ***Robert Gibson*** (1829; after 1850). ***Permelia R.*** (1831; 1916). ***Margaret Bunn*** (1833; before 1850). Watkins and Mary Ann were Quaker South River Monthly Meeting (MM) members in Virginia and moved to Fall Creek MM in Ohio in 1813.

9. Caroline Agnes (9 Sep 1805, Virginia; ?). Caroline was a Quaker South River member in Virginia.

Joseph and Agatha's son Simeon O. Johnson, Madison Center Cemetery, Oskaloosa, Iowa, died age 63.

Simeon had 15 children and died two years after migrating to Iowa in October 1847. His son Wm. Laban erected a marker in Madison Center Cemetery for him and his mother Rachel although Simeon was buried near the school building and Rachel was buried in Silver Creek Cem. Greene co. OH. That memorial stone also mentions Madison their son who was buried "in the wildwood" on the farm where they lived October 1847.

All the children who died young were buried in Silver Creek Cemetery, Greene co. OH along with Rachel and Nancy.

Simeon married (1) Delilah Carroll who died age 26 soon after birth of child, Alfred Carroll Johnson who died age 17

Simeon married 1812 (2) to Nancy Johnson (died age 41), children:

Delilah Albertine Johnson Dalbey (Mrs. Jacob Dalbey)
Emmaline Moriah Johnson died age 16
Carolyn Agnys Johnson died age 21
Charlotte Watkins Johnson died age 1
Arzelia Johnson Wilson(Mrs. Andrew J. Wilson)
Dubys Erskine Johnson died age 1
Martha A. Melvina Johnson Watkins(Mrs. T. T. Watkins) age 20
Eliza Ann Johnson Bryan(Mrs. John Lewis Bryan)

Simeon married 1833 (3) Rachel Cruzen (died age 40), children:

Rachel Ellen "Ellen" Johnson died age 43 single
James Madison "Madison" Johnson died age 11
Simeon Oscar Johnson md. Martha Horner
Isabelle Johnson md. (1) John Watkins, (2) John Latchem (3)Frank Durham
Helen Elizabeth Johnson md. Abraham Bailey
William Laban Johnson md. Abigail Coffin

Simeon married 1845 (4) Eliza Jordan who accompanied him and living family on the migration from Ohio to Mahaska co. IA   —Find A Grave

Left: Joseph and Agatha's grandson Alfred C. Johnson, Old Silvercreek Cemetery, Jamestown, Ohio, died age 17.
Middle: Joseph and Agatha's granddaughter Delilah Johnson Dalbey, Steele Cemetery, Falls City, Nebraska, died age 78.
Right: Joseph and Agatha's granddaughter Emmaline M. Johnson, Old Silvercreek Cemetery, Jamestown, Ohio, died age 16.

Left: Joseph and Agatha's granddaughter Caroline Agnys Johnson, Old Silvercreek Cemetery, Jamestown, Ohio, died age 21.
Middle: Joseph and Agatha's grandson Simeon Oscar Johnson, Summerville Cemetery, Summerville, Oregon, died age 74.
Right: Joseph and Agatha's granddaughter Isabella Johnson Durham, Sumner Cemetery, Sumner, Washington, died age 72.

Left: Joseph and Agatha's granddaughter Helen Elizabeth Johnson Bailey, Madison Cemetery, Oskaloosa, Iowa, died age 81.
Middle: Joseph and Agatha's grandson William Laban Johnson died age 75.
Right: Joseph and Agatha's son Joseph Johnson, Greenwood Cemetery, Galena, Illinois, died age 58.

Joseph and Agatha's grandson Madison Y. Johnson, Greenwood Cemetery, Galena, Illinois, died age 73.

HON. MADISON Y. JOHNSON resides in Galena, Illinois, and is one of the ablest and most successful lawyers in that part of the State. He is a gentleman of fine personal appearance, and about fifty-five years of age. He is independent and self-reliant in his character, but of generous impulses and courteous manners. His arbitrary arrest and imprisonment were, perhaps, among the most the remarkable that occurred during the war, whether considered in a political light, or otherwise, from the fact that he had been the warm personal and political friend of Mr. Lincoln when they were old Whigs together. The personal friendship, which had so long existed between them, was not in the least disturbed up to the time of Mr. Johnson's arrest. . . . He always advocated the doctrine that the theory of American Government was that of consent, and not force. The particular cause of his arrest, or who instigated it, has never been known . . . but it would seem that the act was directed by the President [Lincoln] himself. Mr. Johnson, while engaged in the defence of a murder case, was arrested in open court, on the afternoon of the 28th of August, 1862, by the United States Marshal . . . hurried off, more than a thousand miles, to a foreign State, and incarcerated within the dark walls of the American Bastile . . . confined in what was known as the "Inner Temple," a low, dirty, ill-ventilated room, partially under ground. . . . The order came for Mr. Johnson's discharge . . . if his departure from home was in mystery and silence, his return was in enthusiasm and joy [in December 1862]. —John A. Marshall, *American Bastile,* 1871.

Note: For more in-depth details about the background of Madison Y. Johnson's arrest and imprisonment, access the PDF of this book online. See pages 509–535.

~~~

Katherine "Kitty" Winston Johnson is the Moorman family ancestor. See details in the Paternal Fifth Generation.

~~~

Henry Shaw Elwood

Born 25 Dec 1789 (Franklin, Pennsylvania); died 26 Aug 1863 at age 73 (Marion, Iowa). Buried Pleasant Hill Cemetery, Marion, Iowa. Henry served in the War of 1812.

Henry married (1) Susannah Smalley/Smallie (1790; 1815) on 29 Nov 1814 (Highland, Ohio) when he was 24. They had one son Robert S. Elwood (1815, Ohio; 1900, Red Rock, Iowa) who married Nancy Botts (1824; 1854). They had 1 child Susan Elwood (1842; 1897) married Martin Luther Horn (1837; 1908). It appears the Robert S. Elwood family lived in Marion County, Iowa, near his father, stepmother, and half-siblings.

After Susannah died, Henry married (2) Sarah Sinclair (1798; 1866) on 12 Dec 1816 when he was 26. Sarah probably took on the care of Robert as her first child. Henry and Sarah had 10 children from 1817 to 1840.

Henry Shaw Elwood, Pleasant Hill Cemetery, Red Rock, Iowa, died age 73.

Henry Shaw Elwood's Ancestors beyond Sixth Generation

7. Henry Shaw Elwood's parents were **Robert Elwood** (1751, Armaugh, Northern Ireland; 1818, Highland, Ohio) (see Presbyterian Church Session Records about intoxication, on next page) and **Susan Shaw** (1752, Ireland; 25 Dec 1789, Pennsylvania at the age of 37, perhaps in childbirth, as that is the date her son Henry was born. Robert and Susan married in 1777. They had 7 children in 12 years. They came to the US in the late 1700s. Robert and Susan's parents unknown.

```
Highland Co. Ohio   Rocky springs   Presbyterian Church Session Records
     micro film 859 775

4 Robert Elwood was received into the church on examination   July 3, 1814

5 June 2, 1818
A charge was brought against Robert Elwood, senior, for intoxication  On the
19th or 20th of last may, Robert Elwood, senior, was intoxicated with
spirituous liquor.  He came to the shop of John Hair where James Rogers
and William Steward saw him and he went from that to Daniel Lunbecks.
The charge will be supported by the persons whose names are contained in it.

27 June 25, 1818
Robert Elwood, senior, was cited to attend to answer to the charge of
intoxication, but did not appear.  whereupon the session ordered that he
be cited to attend at this place, the 11th of next July at three o'clock P.M.

8 and 29  July 11, 1818
Mr. Robert Elwood did not appear.  However it being the 3rd time he had been
cited, Session proceeded to take the testimony.  James Rogers being duely
sworn, said that on the day mentioned in the charge, he was in said Hair's
shop, and the accused read up to the door.  He (said Rogers) invited Mr.
Elwood to light and come in out of the rain, but he would not.  He was
full of taulk.  His tongue faltered, so that he could scarcely understand
what he said.  He (the accused) said he was going to Mr. Lunbeck's shop, and
appeared to wish to tel what he was going for, but was incapable, being so
much overcome with liquor.  The manner in which he sat on his horse, impressed
his mind that he had made too free with liquor.  Read and approved by the
witness.                                                               in
Daniel Lunbeck being duely sworn, said Mr. Elwood read up to the bars and
light off his horse.  As he walked to the door, he staggered and when he
came to the door, he (said Lunbeck) smelled liquor on him.  He sat down and
was very taulkative.  He (said Lunbeck) and a Mr Hull who was in the house,
both got tired of his unprofitable chat.  They went to the shop.  Mr.
Elwood went a part of the way with them and then turned and went to the
house where Mrs. Lunbeck was.  The whole of his conduct was that of a man
much the worse of liquor.  Read and approved by the witness.
The session were unanimously of the opinion that the charge was supported
by the testimony.  Whereupon Mr. Robert Elwood, senior, was excluded from
the sealing ordinance of the church until he gives evidence of reformation
and repentance.  And inasmuch as he despises church authority, and has refused
to attend session to answer to the charge, if ever he should offer himself
to the church, he will be to give satisfaction to the church for his
contermucy, before he can enjoy her sealing ordinances.
```

Robert Elwood Sr. Report of Intoxication, Jun and Jul 1818.

~~~

Sarah Sinclair Elwood

Born 14 Feb 1798 (Fayette, Kentucky); died 5 Sep 1866 at age 68 (Marion County, Iowa). Buried Pleasant Hill Cemetery, Red Rock, Iowa. Sarah married Henry Shaw Elwood in 1816 in Ohio.

Sarah Sinclair Elwood, Pleasant Hill Cemetery, Red Rock, Iowa, died age 68.

Sarah Sinclair Elwood's Ancestors beyond Sixth Generation

7. Sarah Sinclair's parents were **John James Stuart Sinclair** (11 Dec 1770, Rowan County, North Carolina; 1824, Ross County, Ohio) and **Sarah Mershon** (1776, Fayette County, Kentucky; Apr 1860, Ross County, Ohio). John and Sarah married 1795 in Fayette, Kentucky. They had 6 children from 1798 to 1816. John was a solider in the War of 1812.

~~~

8. John James Stuart Sinclair's parents were **Amos Sinclair** (1752, Virginia; 14 Aug 1813, Kentucky) and **Mary Margaret Power** (1755, Virginia; 20 May 1816, Kentucky). They had 2 children. Amos served in the Revolutionary War. Amos's mother unknown.

Sarah Mershon's parents were **Andrew Mershon** (1749, New Jersey; 10 Mar 1834, New Jersey) and **Catherine Wilson** (1753, Trenton, New Jersey; 25 Jun 1823, Trenton, New Jersey). Catherine buried at Riverview Cemetery, Trenton, New Jersey. Andrew and Catherine married 15 Oct 1774 (New Jersey). Andrew's parents unknown.

~~~

9. Amos Sinclair's father was **John Sinclair** (1732, Virginia; 26 Jan 1792, Virginia). John James Stuart was named after John Sinclair, his grandfather, a lieutenant who fought under T. Respess in the Virginia Militia in the Revolutionary War, 1777. John's parents unknown.

Mary Margaret Power's parents were **John Power** (1710, Delaware; before 1830, North Carolina) and **Mary Holloway** (1715, Delaware; before 1830, North Carolina). John's and Mary's parents unknown.

Catherine Wilson Mershon's parents were **Peter Wilson** (1716, Monmouth County, New Jersey; 22 Feb 1777, Amwell, New Jersey) and **Hannah Vannoy** (22 Jun 1722, Hopewell, New Jersey; 4 Nov 1806, Hopewell, New Jersey). Peter and Hannah are buried at Pennington Methodist Church Burial Ground, New Jersey. Peter's parents unknown.

~~~

10. Hannah Vannoy's parents were **Francis Vannoy** (15 Sep 1688, Richmond County, New York; Jul 1774, New Jersey) and **Catherine Cornelisse Anderson** (11 Apr 1697, New Jersey; died in childbirth, 14 May 1727, Hopewell, New Jersey). Francis and Catherine married in 1715 (New Jersey) and are buried at Barber Burying Ground, Sandy Ridge, New Jersey.

1768, Aug. 15. Vannoy, Francis, of Hopewell, Hunterdon Co., yeoman; will of. Personal and real estate to be sold, and money given to my 4 children, John Vannoy, Hannah Willson, Cornelius Vannoy and Andrew Vannoy. Eldest son, John, to have £5 more than the rest. Executors—my son, Andrew, and my son-in-law, Peter Willson. Witnesses—Francis Wilson, James Willson, Andrew Willson. Proved July 21, 1774.

1774, July 19. Inventory, £6.7.0, made by Jonathan Hunt and John Heath, Jr. Lib. 16, p. 328.

~~~

11. Francis Vannoy's parents were **John Vannoy** (1644, England; 1699, Staten Island, New York) and **Rachel Cornwall** (1646, England; ?, New York). John and Rachel married ~1684 (England) and are buried at Reformed Church on Staten Island Cemetery, New York. John's and Rachel's parents unknown.

Catherine Anderson's parents were **Cornelius Anderson Sr.** (1670, New Jersey; 1724, New Jersey) and **Annetje Opdyck** (1675, New York; 1746, New Jersey). Cornelius and Annetje married in 1690 (New Jersey) and are buried at First Presbyterian Church of Ewing Cemetery, New Jersey.

~~~

12. Cornelius Anderson Sr.'s parents were **Joachim Andieszen** (~1640, Amsterdam, Netherlands; 11 Mar 1674, New Jersey) and **Emmetje Janszen** (1644, New York; 1674, New York). The name Andieszen was later changed to Anderson. Joachim's and Emmetje's parents unknown.

Annetje Opdyck's parents were **Johannes Lourense Opdyck** (1651; 1729, New Jersey) and **Catherine Trintye** (1655, New York; 3 Mar 1746, New Jersey). Catherine's parents unknown.

~~~

13. Johannes Opdyck's parents were **Louris Jansen Opdyke** (1620, Netherlands; 1659, New York) and **Stijntje "Christina" Pieters** (1622, Netherlands; 16 Mar 1693, New Jersey). Louris is buried in Gravesend Cemetery, Brooklyn, New York. Louris's and Stijntje's parents unknown.

~~~

Henry and Sarah Elwood Summary

Henry Shaw Elwood (26) and Sarah Sinclair (18) married in 1816 (Highland County, Ohio). They had 10 children in 23 years.

1. **George Washington** (14 Oct 1817, Martinsville, Ohio; 1877, Prairie City, Iowa) married (1) Narcissa Shockley on 3 Sep 1842 (Ohio). They had 2 children. George married (2) Sarah Jane Botts (1828; 1882) on 2 Apr 1849 (Iowa). They had 10 children. See details in Paternal Fifth Generation.

2. **Mahala** (31 Oct 1817, Martinsville, Ohio; 28 Oct 1906, David City, Nebraska; buried Brainard IOOF Cemetery, Nebraska) married Nathan Moon (1819; 1888) on 24 Feb 1841 (Ohio). Nathan served in the US Civil War. They had 3 children: *John* (1845; 1920), *Alonzo D.* (1853; 1948), *Mary E.* (1856; 1936).

3. **John Sinclair** (2 Nov 1822, Ohio; 1900, Reno County, Kansas; buried Sego Cemetery, Pretty Prairie, Kansas) married Eliza E. Hodson (1832; 1893) in 1848 (Ohio). They had 11 children: *James Edwin* (1852; 1931), *Mary Delcenia* (1854; 1929); *Columbus Americus* (1856; 1932), *Jasper Newton* (1857; 1941), *Henry Shaw* (1859; 1881), *John William* (1861; 1881), *Eliza Ellen* (1864; 1948), *Robert Hodson* (1867; 1939), *Harley* (1871; 1916), *Mattie Evaleen* (1879; 1977).

4. **Hiram William** (17 May 1825, Hillsboro, Ohio; 3 Mar 1894, Norfolk, Nebraska; buried Greenwood Cemetery, Creighton, Nebraska) married (1) Cynthia A. Botts (1827; 1860) in 1847. They had 7 children: *Mary E.* (1848; 1874), *Nathan* (1850; 1929), *Elvira Jane* (1852; 1935), *James N.* (1854; 1919), *Silvanus* (1855; 1939), *Henry Clay* (1857; 1950), *Mahala Emily* (1860; 1919). Hiram married (2) Susan Pickering Hockette (1818; 1903) in 1862. She had 3 children from a previous marriage.

Obituary—H. W. Elwood, aged 60, a patient at the asylum, died last evening. The remains were sent to friends in Creighton on the 2:20 train. —*Norfolk Daily News*, Nebraska, 3 Mar 1894.

5. Azariah Sinclair, Dr. (29 Oct 1827, New Petersburg, Ohio; 26 Mar 1906, Denver, Colorado; buried Fairmount Cemetery, Denver, Colorado) married (1) Elvira Jane Cowman (1835; 1853) on 14 Oct 1852 (Marion, Iowa). They had 1 child: *Frances* (1853; 1853) died 24 days. Azariah married (2) Mary Elizabeth Howard (1843; 1928) in 1861. They had 3 children: *Martha "Mattie" Elizabeth* (1863; 1927); *William Henry* (1866; 1961) mined in Colorado and drove stagecoach out of Cripple Creek, Colorado; *Charles "Charlie" S.* (1869; 1870). A. S. served in the US Civil War from 13 Sep 1862 until 14 Oct 1863. He was a private in the Union, Company E, 40th Iowa Infantry and served as assistant surgeon. He participated in the siege of Vicksburg and served in Kentucky with the Tenth Missouri Cavalry. He was honorably discharged with a disability due to overwork and overexposure. After the war, A.S. was a doctor in Monroe, Iowa; Golden, Colorado; and Denver, Colorado.

6. William J. (11 Jul 1832, Ohio; 28 May 1910, Nebraska) married Mary Emily Smith (1838; 1925) on 22 Aug 1856 (Marion, Iowa). They had 8 children: *Azariah S.* (1858; 1938), *Victoria* (1860; 1938), *John Irving* (1862; 1937), *Henry S.* (1865; after 1938), *Laura* (1869; after 1870), *Lula/Lulu* (1871; 1957), *Hiram* (1877; 1949), *Ethelynn F.* (1880; 1966).

7. Henry (1833; 1833).

8. Elizabeth (1834; 1842) died age 8.

9. James Amos (10 Jan 1837, Ohio; 17 Mar 1919, Rice County, Minnesota; buried Grove Lake Cemetery, Pope County, Minnesota) married Margaret Cowman (1843; 1913) on 24 Jul 1857 (Marion, Iowa). They had 11 children. *Eldora Francis* (1859; 1918), *Sarah Rebecca* (1862; 1899), *Alvy* (1863; 1898), *William Henry* (1864; 1944), *Cora Francis* (1866; 1937), *Joseph Cary* (1870; 1940), *Sherman Floyd* (1874; 1967), *Gertrude Luina* (1877; 1968), *Cassius Henry* (1882; 1956), *Alva Franklin* (1882; 1898), *Mary Elizabeth* (1886; 1970).

10. Nancy E. (1840, Ohio; 20 Oct 1880, Jasper County, Iowa; buried Monroe Cemetery, Monroe, Iowa) married Henry Rater (~1837, Germany, ?) on 19 Feb 1880 (Marion, Iowa). Nancy died 6 months later.

~~~

Left: Henry and Sarah Elwood's daughter Mahala Elwood Moon, Brainard IOOF Cemetery, Nebraska, died age 88. Middle and right: Henry and Sarah Elwood's son John died age 77 and spouse Eliza Elwood died age 60, Sego Cemetery, Pretty Prairie, Kansas.

Left: Henry and Sarah Elwood's grandson James Edwin Elwood and spouse Mary. Unknown child.
Right: Henry and Sarah's grandsons Columbus Americus Elwood and Jasper Newton Elwood.

Left and middle: Henry and Sarah Elwood's son Hiram W. Elwood (with spouse Susan), Greenwood Cemetery,
Creighton, Nebraska, died age 68. Susan is buried at Hill City Cemetery, Hill City, Kansas.
Right: Henry and Sarah Elwood's son Hiram W. Elwood and his spouse Susan, near Creighton, Nebraska.

Henry and Sarah Elwood's grandchildren, Hiram's children: Nathan, Elvira, Silvanus, Henry, Mahala.

Henry and Sarah Elwood's son A. S. Elwood. Left: A. S. Elwood, Civil War uniform.
Right: Martha "Mattie" Elizabeth, Azariah, William Henry, and Mary Elizabeth Howard Elwood, ~1870.

Henry and Sarah Elwood's son A. S. Elwood, MD.

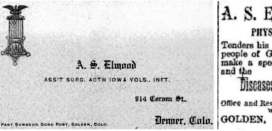

A. S. Elwood business card and advertisement.

Left: Henry and Sarah Elwood's son A. S. Elwood, Fairmount Cemetery, Denver, Colorado, died age 78.
Right: Henry and Sarah Elwood's son William J. Elwood, Wyuka Cemetery, Lincoln, Nebraska died age 78.

Left: Henry and Sarah Elwood's granddaughter Cora Francis Elwood. Middle: Henry and Sarah Elwood's daughter-in-law Margaret Cowman Elwood, grandson Alva Franklin Elwood, and son James Amos Elwood. Right: Henry and Sarah Shaw's granddaughter Mary Elizabeth and spouse Clarence Elmer Reed.

~~~

In the **1850 US Census,** Henry Elwood (63) is listed as a farmer, living in Marion County, Iowa, with Sarah (53), Azariah (22) a farmer, William (18) a farmer, James A. (13), and Nancy E. (10).

In the **1850 US Non-Population Schedule,** Henry Elwood is listed as living in Marion County, Iowa, and having 60 acres of improved acres of land and 120 acres of unimproved land. The cash value of his farm was $2300 and the value of the farm implements was $200. He had 4 horses, 2 milch cows, 3 other cattle, 13 sheep, 60 swine. The value of the livestock was $2000. Also listed was 40 bushels of wheat, 350 bushels of Indian corn, 135 bushels of oats, 20 pounds of wool, 4 bushels of sweet potatoes, 300 pounds of butter, and 1 ton of hay.

In the **1856 Iowa Census,** Henry Elwood (68) is listed as a farmer, living in Des Moines with Sarah (56), William (23), James A. (18), and Nancy E. (16).

In the **1860 US Census,** Henry Elwood (69) is listed as a farmer, living in Des Moines with Sarah (55).

~~~

George Washington Elwood is the Moorman family ancestor. See details in the Paternal Fifth Generation.

~~~

Benjamin Shockley

Born 4 Oct 1780 (Worcester County, Maryland); died 5 Nov 1849 at age 69 (Henry County, Iowa); buried Hochreiter Cemetery (Henry County, Iowa). Married Sally Melson on 25 Feb 1804 (Worcester, Maryland). His death at the age of 69 was caused by diarrhea.

Benjamin Shockley, Hochreiter Cemetery, Iowa, died age 69.

Benjamin Shockley's Ancestors beyond Sixth Generation

7. Benjamin Shockley's parents were **Benjamin Sampson Shockley** (4 Jul 1731, Stepney Parish, Somerset, Maryland; 4 Dec 1798, Worcester County, Maryland) and **Elizabeth Smith** (1748; 1814). Married 1773 (Worcester, Maryland). They had 6 children. Benjamin Sampson's mother unknown.

~~~

8. Benjamin Sampson Shockley's father was **Richard I. Shockley III** (1 Jun 1677, Manoakin, Maryland; 13 Aug 1741, Kent County, Delaware).

Elizabeth Smith's parents were **Archibald Smith** (7 Oct 1717, Somerset County, Maryland; 3 Jun 1761, Worcester County, Maryland) and **Tarna Turner** (1724, Maryland; 1752, Somme, Picardie, France). They had 9 children. Tarna's parents unknown.

~~~

9. Richard I. Shockley III's parents were **Richard Shockley** (no details) and **Ann** (no details).

Archibald Smith's parents were **George Smith** (1650, England; 21 Aug 1717, Somerset County, Maryland) and **Sarah Ann Cox** (1680, Maryland; before 1761, Maryland). George and Sarah married in 1700. They had 6 children. Sarah's parents unknown.

~~~

10. George Smith's parents were **James Smith** (1620, England; 1693, England) and **Mariam Smith** (1620, England; ?). James and Mariam married in 1645. James's and Mariam's parents unknown.

~~~

Sally Melson Shockley

Born 12 Mar 1787 (Maryland); died 23 Jul 1847 at age (Henry County, Iowa); buried Hochreiter Cemetery (Henry County, Iowa). Married Benjamin Shockley on 25 Feb 1804 (Worcester, Maryland). They had 19 children in 28 years. Sally died of apoplexy.

"Salley" Melson Shockley Hochreiter Cemetery, Iowa, died age 60.

Sally Melson Shockley's Ancestors beyond Sixth Generation

7. Sally Melson's parents were **Elijah Melson** (1762, Little Creek Hundred, Delaware; 7 Mar 1824, Melson, Maryland) and **Mary Polly Hearne** (1766, Little Creek Hundred, Delaware; 12 Jan 1816, Melson, Maryland). Elijah and Polly married in 1784 (Sussex County, Delaware). They had 7 children.

~~~

8. Elijah Melson's parents were **Daniel Melson** (1724, Accomack County, Virginia; 2 Oct 1797, Broadcreek Hundred, Sussex, Delaware) and **Lovey Cannon** (1737, Somerset, Maryland; after 4 Dec 1798, Little Creek Hundred, Delaware). Daniel served as a private on the Union side of the US Civil War: 1st Regiment, Maryland Eastern Shore Infantry, Company D. He owned over 600 acres in Delaware and Maryland. Daniel and Lovey married about 1744. They had 10 children. Lovey's parents unknown.

Mary Polly Hearne's parents were **Samuel Hearne** (1730, Delmar, Delaware; Jun 1803, Somerset, Maryland) and **Elizabeth Methvin** (1730, Delmar, Delaware; 1785, Somerset, Maryland). Samuel and Elizabeth had 5 children. Samuel's and Elizabeth's parents unknown.

~~~

9. Daniel Melson's parents were **Daniel Melson** (1707, Hunting Creek, Virginia; 20 Apr 1791, Wicomico Hundred, Maryland) and **Mary Cary** (1710, Hunting Creek, Virginia; after 20 Apr 1791, Wicomico Hundred, Maryland). Daniel and Mary married in 1722. They had 6 children.

~~~

10. Daniel Melson's parents were **John Melson** (1670, Virginia; 1737, Virginia) and **Mary Douglas Smith** (1677, Virginia; 1743, Virginia). John and Mary married in 1695 (Virginia). They had 11 children.

Mary Cary's parents were **Solomon Cary** (1674, Virginia; 1750, Virginia) and **Margaret** (1678; ?). Margaret's parents unknown.

~~~

11. John Melson's parents were **John Melson** (1646, Yorkshire, England; 1687, Virginia) and **Elizabeth Painter** (1648, England; 2 Dec 1691, Virginia). John and Elizabeth married in 1671 (Maryland). They had 5 children. John's and Elizabeth's parents unknown.

Mary Douglas Smith's parents were **Joshua Smith** (1647, England; 14 Nov 1683, Virginia) and **Margaret Ann Abraham** (1650, Virginia; 1683, ?). Joshua and Margaret married in 1670 (Virginia). They had 4 children. Margaret's parents unknown.

Solomon Cary's parents were **John Cary** (4 Nov 1645, England; May 1701, Virginia) and **Elizabeth Godfrey** (1646, Virginia; 1680, Massachusetts). John and Elizabeth's parents unknown.

~~~

12. Joshua Smith's parents were **John Richard Smith** (1625, Norfolk, England; 27 Apr 1695, Massachusetts or Virginia) and **Bridgett Small** (1621, England; ?). John's and Bridgett's parents unknown.

~~~

Benjamin and Sally Shockley Summary

Benjamin Shockley (23) and Sally Melson (16) married on 25 Feb 1804 (Worcester, Maryland). They had 19 children in 28 years.

1. Samuel (13 Feb 1805; ?).

2. Elizabeth (6 Oct 1806; 1808).

3. Sampson (~1809, Highland County, Ohio; 4 Dec 1898, Carthage, Missouri) brick mason, married (1) Abigail Clark (1812; 1835) on 28 Oct 1830 (Ohio). They had 2 children: *Andrew Jackson* (1828; 1882), *Milligen/Millican* (1832; after 1864) mason, served in the US Civil War, private, Company A, 17th Illinois Infantry (1861–1864). Sampson married (2) Elizabeth Humphrey (1823; 1896) on 6 Sep 1836 (Ohio). They had 7 children: *Thomas U.* (1838; 1897), *Mary J.* (1840; after 1860), *Sarah Ann* (1842; 1912), *Martha E.* (1843; 1945), *Charles N.* (1851; 1922), *Benjamin* (1855; 1949), *Ida Josephine* (1859; 1895).

4. Nancy (1810, Highland County, Ohio; ?).

5. William (25 Nov 1810, Ross County, Ohio; 10 Aug 1886, Hartford, Kansas; buried Hartford Cemetery, Hartford, Kansas) married Mary B. Anderson (1814; 1891) in 1836 (Ohio). They had 8 children, 2 survived to adulthood: *Elizabeth "Eliza" H.* (1838; 1920), *Sally* (~1843; after 1860).

6. Elijah (20 Mar 1812, Ross County, Ohio; 25 Nov 1848, Keokuk County, Iowa) married Martha W. Hood (1819; 1858) in 1834 (Ohio). They had 9 children: *Jane* (1834; 1856); *Benjamin E.* (1835; 1863) doctor and private in US Civil War; *Margaret Jane* (1836; 1859); *William C.* (1837; 1918) private in US Civil War, Company F, Iowa 5th Cavalry; *Samuel M.* (1840; 1911) US Civil War. Iowa 8th Infantry; *Emily P.* (1841; 1841); *Thomas A.* (1842; 1863) private US Civil War, Iowa 5th Infantry, killed in battle at Missionary Ridge, Chattanooga, Tennessee; *Celia N.* (1843; 1909); *Sarah Elizabeth* (1847; 1939).

7. Joanne (1814, Highland County, Ohio; 1865, Springfield, Illinois) married Augustus Brown Jewett (1810; 1855) on 9 Apr 1832 (Ohio). They had 7 children: *Collins M.* (1833; after 1850), *Cynthann* (1836; 1855), *Christopher Columbus* (1838; 1906) served in the US Civil War, 2nd Illinois Cavalry, *Samantha Jane* (1842; 1863), *James Brown* (1845; after 1860), *Elizabeth Mae* (1847; 1869), *Harriet Levina* (after 1850; ?). After Augustus died in 1855, Joanne and the children moved to Illinois.

8. Archibald (22 Mar 1815, Ross County, Ohio; 24 Oct 1889, Covington, Indiana).

9. Enoch (1815, Highland County, Ohio; Jan 1850, Oneco, Illinois; buried Mount Pleasant Cemetery, Oneco, Illinois) farmer, married Malinda Walton (1823; 1888) on 17 Mar 1847 (Illinois). They had 2 children: *Margaret J.* (1847; after 1918), *Sarah Anne* (1850; 1927). Enoch died of consumption.

10. Thomas (16 Apr 1817, Ross County, Ohio; 10 Feb 1871, Lyon County, Kansas; buried Americus Cemetery, Kansas) brick mason, married Asenath Shockley (1815; 1880) in 1837 (Ohio). They had 5 children: **Albert D.** (1840; 1939) a reverend and US Civil War veteran, **Elizabeth** (~1843; after 1850), **John** (~1843; after 1850), **Louisa Ellen** (1843; 1899), **Mary Izabell** (1850; 1939). Thomas and Asenath moved to Iowa and were listed there in the 1850 US Census. Thomas served in the US Civil War, private, Company B, 3rd Illinois Cavalry (1861–1864). Discharged for disability (wounds) 7 Mar 1862.

11. Mary (21 Jan 1819, Ross County, Ohio; 1867).

12. Benjamin P. (Apr 1820, Highland County, Ohio; 15 Jun 1883, Green City, Missouri) farmer, married Abigail Hart (1824; 1882) in 1840. They had 6 children: *Wilson S.* (1843; 1927), *Louisa S.* (1849; 1940), *Thomas W.* (1856; 1865), *James R.* (1858; 1953), *Abbie Jane* (1864; 1945), *Benjamin F.* (1865; 1942).

13. John Denis (5 Jan 1821, Ross County, Ohio; 31 Jan 1892, Clear Creek, Iowa; buried Shockley Cemetery, Keokuk County, Iowa) married Elizabeth Hornish (1823; 1896). They had 10 children: **William** (~1846; after 1860), **Mary Ann** (1848; 1892), **Charles Ira** (1850; 1923), **George N.** (~1854; after 1880), **John M.** (1856; 1881), **Sarah Ella** (1858; 1885), **Clara Bell** (1860; 1920), **Ida M.** (1862; 1881), **Laura Ella** (~1867; after 1880), **Hattie Eldora** (1868; 1939).

14. Seth (1822, Ross County, Ohio; 1822, Ross County, Ohio) died at birth.

15. Sarah D. (29 Apr 1824, Ross County, Ohio; 4 Jun 1915, Los Angeles, California; buried Angelus Rosedale Cemetery, Los Angeles, California) married Thomas W. Alexander (1819; 1888) on 25 Jan 1843 (Ross County, Ohio). They had 5 children: *Mary Ann* (1850; 1930), *William Latta* (1851; 1921), *Robert Benjamin* (1858; 1931), *Charles W.* (1861; 1862), *Laura Alice* (1863; 1889).

16. Narcissa (~1824, Highland County, Ohio; ~1846, Ohio) married George W. Elwood on 3 Sep 1842 (Clinton, Ohio). They had 2 children. See details in Paternal Fifth Generation.

17. Andrew Jackson (~1826, Ross County, Ohio; 1826, Ross County, Ohio) died at birth.

18. Celia Williams (15 Sep 1826, Ross County, Ohio; 15 Sep 1871, Henry County, Iowa; buried North Wayne Cemetery, Olds, Iowa) married Edward Smith (1820; 1882) in 1846. They had 8 children: *George Dexter* (1847; 1919) Norfolk, Nebraska, businessman, farmer, active in politics; *William* (1849; after 1860); *Sarah* (1852; after 1860); *Ethan* (~1853; after 1860); *Clara Ellen* (1855; 1926); *Emma* (~1856; after 1860); *Sylvester Clark* (1858; 1913) newspaper owner/editor, attorney, California congressman for four terms; *Edward Parsons* (1860; 1930), mayor of Omaha, Nebraska (1918–1921).

19. George Washington (9 Feb 1833, Ross County, Ohio; 31 Dec 1865, Knoxville, Tennessee) married Elizabeth "Eliza" Jane Wilson (1833; 1904) on 3 Jul 1853 (Iowa). They had 3 children: *John F.* (1855; 1897), *Edward W.* (1859; 1918), *Sarah Ella* (1862; 1928). George served on the Union side in the US Civil War. Enlisted 20 Jun 1863 in Ohio; private in K Company, 2nd HA Artillery. Mustered out 23 Aug 1865, Nashville, Tennessee.

~~~

Benjamin and Sally's son Sampson Shockley and spouse Elizabeth.

Benjamin and Sally's grandson Andrew Jackson Shockley

Andrew Jackson Shockley was baptized a member of the Reorganized Church of Jesus Christ of Latter Day Saints on 9 January 1870 at Canton, Lee, Iowa, by R. Warnock. He died while working on the Fort Medicine and Northwestern Railroad, when the flatcar he was on left the track, turned over, and crushed him. —Early Reorganization Minutes, 1852-1871, Book A, p. 505/ *Saints' Herald* Obituaries, 1882, p. 160/ Early Reorganization Minutes, 1872-1905, Book B

Benjamin and Sally's son William Shockley

Wm. Shockley died in the 78th year of his age at Hartford yesterday. He is one of the oldest settlers in the county, having lived here thirty years. The funeral took place to-day at 2 o'clock. The remains were laid to rest in the Hartford cemetery.

—*The Emporia Daily News*, 11 Aug 1886, Wednesday

Left: Benjamin and Sarah's son Elijah Shockley.
Middle and right: Benjamin and Sarah's granddaughter Sarah Elizabeth Shockley Boyer. Right: circa 1918.

Left: Benjamin and Sarah's grandson Christopher C. Jewett and spouse Miranda.
Right: Benjamin and Sarah's son Enoch Shockley, Mount Pleasant Cemetery, Oneco, Illinois, died age 36.

Left: Benjamin and Sarah's granddaughter Sarah Anne Shockley Pritchett.
Right: Sarah and her mother Malinda Walton Shockley, circa 1870–1888.

Left: Benjamin and Sarah's daughter Sarah Alexander, Angelus Rosedale Cemetery, Los Angeles, California, died age 91.
Right: Benjamin and Sarah's daughter Celia W. Shockley Smith, North Wayne Cemetery, Olds, Iowa, died age 37.

Benjamin and Sarah's grandsons George Dexter Smith, Sylvester Clark Smith, Edward Parsons Smith.

~~~

In the **1820 US Census,** Benjamin Shockley was living in Union, Ohio. There were 10 persons in the household: 4 males under 10, 1 male 10-15, 1 adult male, 2 females under 10, 1 female 10-15, 1 adult female.

In the **1830 US Census,** "Benjn" Shockley was living in Deerfield, Ohio. There were 11 persons in the household: 1 male 5-9, 1 male 10-14, 3 males 15-19, 1 adult male, 1 female under 5, 1 female 5-9, 1 female 10-14, 2 females over 30.

~~~

Narcissa Shockley Elwood is the Moorman family ancestor. See details in the Paternal Fifth Generation.

~~~

Summary of Paternal Fifth Generation

William Moorman was born in Virginia and died age 77 in Iowa. He was a Quaker. Williams's paternal grandfather (Micajah Moorman) and maternal grandmother (Agatha Agness Moorman) were brother and sister.

Katherine "Kitty" Winston Johnson Moorman was born in Virginia and died age 76 in Iowa.

William (26) and Kitty Johnson (20) married in 1817 (Virginia). They had 10 children in 23 years.

Edwin Moorman is the Moorman family ancestor. See details in the Paternal Fourth Generation.

~~~

George Washington Elwood was born in Iowa and died age 60 in Iowa. He was married twice and had a total of 12 children. In 1863, George (43) and his brother John (41) were listed in the US Civil War Registration Records, both were living in Des Moines, and they were listed as farmers.

Narcissa Shockley Elwood was born in Ohio and died age 23 in Ohio. When Narcissa died, she left her spouse and two daughters (ages 3 and 1).

George (25) and Narcissa (18) married in 1842 (Ohio). They had 2 children in 2 years.

Mahala "Hallie" Jane Elwood Moorman is the Moorman family ancestor. See details in the Paternal Fourth Generation.

~~~

William Moorman

Born 8 Mar 1792 (Lynchburg, Virginia); died 8 Jan 1870 at age 77 (Pleasant Plain, Iowa). Buried Friends Cemetery (Pleasant Plain, Iowa). Married Kitty Johnson on 29 Jan 1817 (Fairfield, Ohio). Williams's paternal grandfather (Micajah Moorman) and maternal grandmother (Agatha Moorman, born 1749) were brother and sister. His wife's maternal grandfather was Zachariah Moorman, a brother to Micajah and Agatha.

> I never saw my great grandfather, Bill Moorman, or my great grandmother [Kitty], but I have heard from very interesting stories about them. Bill was a gunsmith by trade. He and grandmother settled in Washington County near Richland, Iowa in the 1840s with their family of five girls and four boys. There they raised their family. During the Civil War the family was divided, half for the North and half for the South. One of the brothers [John Winston?] organized a company of Confederate cavalry, had their uniforms smuggled across the lines and rode into town hoping to get more volunteers. When one of the brothers [Joseph or William?] whose sympathy was with the North came out of a pool hall and saw his brother dressed in a Confederate uniform and with a captain's commission, he pulled a revolver from his holster and shot and killed his own brother. My grandfather [Edwin] who was the captain of the minute men called his men together and ambushed the rest of that gang as they were crossing at a ford of the Skunk River. They killed all but one. —From *Wa du ya no bout Us*[3]

~~~

Katherine "Kitty" Winston Johnson

Born 15 Mar 1798 (Bedford County, Virginia); died 6 Jul 1874 at age 76 (Pleasant Plain, Iowa). Buried Friends Cemetery (Pleasant Plain, Iowa). Married William Moorman on 29 Jan 1817 (Fairfield, Ohio).

~~~

William and Kitty Moorman Summary

William Moorman (26) and Katherine "Kitty" Winston Johnson (20) married in 1817 (Fairfield, Ohio). They were both Quakers. They had 10 children in 23 years. William and Kitty were originally part of the Quakers South River Monthly Meeting, Lynchburg City, Virginia. The family was granted certificate to (gct) the Pleasant Plain, Iowa, Monthly Meeting on 15 Nov 1845.

> During the nine years from 1842 to 1850 one hundred and fifty members came from various Quaker centers in Ohio, Indiana, North Carolina, and Tennessee. Again the movement pressed onward, finding its way into Keokuk County, where P. C. Woodward, with the Bray, Williams, Haworth, Moorman, Hadley, and other Quaker families quickly built up the thriving communities of Richland and Rocky Run.

—The Quakers of Iowa

1. Joseph Watkins (19 Jan 1818, Ohio; died after 1885) Quaker, married (1) Deliza "Eliza" Burger (1825; 1884) on 10 Jul 1842 (Ohio). They had 2 children: ***Addison*** (1844; 1916), ***Sarah Elizabeth*** (1845; 1932). After Deliza died in 1884, Joseph married (2) Lavina Petit Thompson (1830; after 1885) on 22 Sep 1885 (Decatur, Iowa). They had no children. The **1850 US Census** lists home as Mahaska, Iowa, Joseph's occupation was "shoe maker." In the **1860 and 1870 US Census**, they lived in Richland, Iowa, and Joseph's occupation was "cabinet maker." In th **1880 US Census**, they lived in Eddyville, Iowa, and Joseph's occupation was cabinet maker.

2. Collins (16 Sep 1819, Ohio; 19 Feb 1821, Ohio; buried Fairfield, Ohio) Quaker, died age 1.

3. Emily (19 Dec 1821, Ohio; 22 Apr 1865, Iowa; buried Friends Cemetery, Pleasant Plain, Iowa) Quaker, married Addison Johnson (1819; 1898) Quaker. They had 5 children: ***Lindley*** (1843; 1851), ***Aquilla*** (1845; 1847), ***Sarah*** (1848; 1858), ***Eunice*** (1853; after 1870), ***Horace*** (1854; after 1870).

4. Nancy Catherine (31 Aug 1824, Ohio; 6 Sep 1873, Lowell, Kansas) Quaker, married John Bell (1826; 1887) on 2 Dec 1846 (Pleasant Plain, Iowa). They had 8 children: ***Alexander W.*** (1848; 1887), ***Martha Ellen*** (1849; 1887), ***Emily*** (1851; 1887), ***Jannette*** (1853; 1854), ***William*** (1856; 1857), ***Oscar Haywood*** (1858; 1937), ***Arthur Fremont*** (1860; 1872), ***Mary Frances*** (1863; 1872). In the **1860 US Census,** they lived in Richland, Iowa.

---

[3] Erwin and Ethel Moorman, *Wa du ya no bout Us,* 1979. Copy in possession of editor of this book.

5. Elizabeth (20 Apr 1827, Ohio; 21 Jan 1848, Iowa; buried Friends Cemetery, Pleasant Plain, Iowa) Quaker, died age 20.

6. Edwin (25 Oct 1832, Ohio; 13 Aug 1909, Knob Noster, Missouri; buried Knob Noster Cemetery, Missouri) Quaker, married Mahala "Hallie" Jane Elwood (1844; 1922) on 16 Dec 1862 (Pleasant Plain, Iowa). They had 9 children. See details in Paternal Fourth Generation. Three brothers—Edwin, W.T., Jno—registered for the US Civil War draft in Iowa on 20 Jul 1863.

7. William Thomas (20 Mar 1835, Ohio; 9 Jul 1904, Delta, Washington; buried Lynden Cemetery, Washington) Quaker. In 1848, William was "dis" disowned for unbecoming conduct toward a female. According to the Civil War registration, William was unmarried in 1863. In the **1870 US Census,** William and his mother Kitty lived in Penn, Iowa. In the **1900 US Census,** William (65) is listed as single, living in Delta, Washington. He died age 69 of pneumonia.

8. Mary Agnes, twin (15 Dec 1837, Ohio; 15 Apr 1921, Hardin, Montana) Quaker, married Enos Clark Hobson (1833; 1889) Quaker, on 14 Sep 1853 (Pleasant Plain, Iowa). Enos was a US Civil War veteran. They had 4 children: ***George Arnett*** (1854; 1934), ***Ella*** (1857; 1944), ***Alfred Enos "Fred"*** (1859; 1939), ***John*** (1861; 1944). In 1900, Mary, widowed, lived in Richland, Iowa. In 1910, she lived in Yellowstone, Montana. In 1912, she lived in Billings, Montana.

9. Lydia Ann, twin (15 Dec 1837, Ohio; 9 Jan 1917, Coulee City, Washington; buried Saint Andrews Cemetery, Douglas County, Washington) Quaker, married William Zeno Hobson, MD (1822; 1896) Quaker, on 15 Sep 1852 (Pleasant Plain, Iowa). They had 5 children: ***Mary*** (1854; after 1860), ***Charles*** (1856; 1901), ***William*** (1858; after 1870), ***Lucy Ann*** (1861; 1948), ***Lydia Bessie*** (1869; 1872). In the **1900 US Census,** Lydia lived with her son Charles in Chelan, Washington. NOTE: Twins Mary Agnes and Lydia Ann married brothers Enos Hobson and Zeno Hobson.

10. John Winston (10 Jul 1841, Ohio; 16 Dec 1863; buried Friends Cemetery, Pleasant Plain, Iowa) Quaker, farmer, died age 22.

~~~

William and Kitty's son William Thomas Moorman, Lynden Cemetery, Washington, died age 69.

William and Kitty's daughter Mary Agnes Moorman Hobson.

William and Kitty's grandson Fred Hobson. Left: Richland, Iowa. Right: Montana.

Original Record for State Registrar

THE DEMOCRAT, LEWISTOWN, MONT.

STATE OF MONTANA
Bureau of Vital Statistics
Standard Certificate of Death

Yel. 1991
Do not write in this space

1. PLACE OF DEATH
County Yellowstone Registered No. 346
Township or Village
City Billings No. Yellowstone County Farm St., Ward
(If death occurred in a hospital or institution, give its NAME instead of street and number)
Length of residence in city or town where death occurred 35 yrs. mos. days. How long in U. S. if of foreign birth? yrs. mos. days

2. FULL NAME Fred Hobson
(a) Residence: No. Billings, Mont. St., Ward.
(Usual place of abode) (If nonresident give city or town and State)

PERSONAL AND STATISTICAL PARTICULARS

3. SEX Male
4. COLOR OR RACE white
5. SINGLE, MARRIED, WIDOWED, OR DIVORCED (write the word) widowed

5a. If married, widowed, or divorced HUSBAND of (or) WIFE of

6. DATE OF BIRTH (month, day, and year) April 1, 1857

7. AGE Years 82 Months 5 Days 29 If LESS than 1 day, hrs. or min.

8. Trade, profession, or particular kind of work done, as spinner, sawyer, bookkeeper, etc. Farmer
9. Industry or business in which work was done, as silk mill, saw mill, bank, etc.
10. Date deceased last worked at this occupation, (month and year)
11. Total time (years) spent in this occupation

12. BIRTHPLACE (city or town) Pleasant Plain (State or country) Iowa
13. NAME Enos Clark Hobson
14. BIRTHPLACE (city or town) Indiana (State or country)
15. MAIDEN NAME Mary Agnes Moorman
16. BIRTHPLACE (city or town) Ohio
17. INFORMANT Mrs. Art Bellin (Address) Route 2, Idaho Falls, Idaho
18. BURIAL, CREMATION, OR REMOVAL Place Hardin, Mont. Date Oct. 3 39
19. UNDERTAKER G. Herman Smith (Address) Billings, Mont.
20. FILED 10-2, 19 39 Registrar

MEDICAL CERTIFICATE OF DEATH

21. DATE OF DEATH (month, day, and year) Sept. 30, 1939
22. I HEREBY CERTIFY, That I attended deceased from , 19 , to , 19 .
I last saw him alive on , 19 , death is said to have occurred on the date stated above, at 5:30PM m.
The principal cause of death and related causes of importance in order of onset were as follows:
Suicide Date of onset 9/30/39
Skull Fracture
(169)
Contributory causes of importance not related to principal cause:

Name of operation , Date of .
What test confirmed diagnosis? Was there an autopsy? no
23. If death was due to external causes (violence) fill in also the following:
Accident, suicide, or homicide? Suicide Date of injury 9, 30, 1938
Where did injury occur? Billings Yel. Mont.
(Specify city or town, county, and State)
Specify whether injury occurred in industry, in home, or in public place.
Public place- Yel. Co. Farm
Manner of injury Jumped from 2nd story window
Nature of injury Fractured skull
24. Was disease or injury in any way related to occupation of deceased? no
If so, specify
(Signed) Howard C. Smith (coroner) M. D.
(Address) Billings, Mont.

William and Kitty's grandson Fred Hobson death certificate, died age 82. Committed suicide by jumping from a second-story window at Yellowstone County Farm—a public place—fractured his skull.

William and Kitty's daughter Lydia Ann Moorman Hobson, Saint Andrews Cemetery, Douglas County, Washington, died age 79.

Left to right - Lucy A. McClellan, Claude, William S.
McClellan. Bottom row - Jessie, Clifford & Minnie
June. Picture taken approx. 1888 to 1890 in Brighton
Iowa prior to leaving for Washington Territory. (Note:
Nellie was born in Coulee City, WA 11 Dec 1890)

William and Kitty's granddaughter Lucy Ann Hobson McClellan family, ~1889, Brighton, Iowa.

~~~

In the **1850 US Census,** "Wm Moman" is listed as a farmer in Penn, Jefferson County, Iowa. He was living with his spouse "Catharine" and 5 children: Edwin (18), Wm (15), Mary (13), Lydia (13), and John (7).

In the **1856 Iowa Census,** "Walliam" and Kitty lived in Penn, Jefferson County, Iowa, with William S. Moorman (21) and John W. Moorman (14). William's occupation listed as "peddler."

In the **1860 US Census,** William "Moorron" is listed as a farmer in Penn, Jefferson County, Iowa. He was living with his spouse Kitty and 3 children: Edwin (27), William T. (25), and John W. (7).

In the **1870 US Census,** the residence is listed as Penn, Jefferson County, Iowa. "Ritty" (72) lives with William (35).

~~~

Edwin Moorman is the Moorman family ancestor. See details in the Paternal Fourth Generation.

~~~

George Washington Elwood

Born 14 Oct 1817 (Martinsville, Ohio); died 1877 at age 60 (Prairie City, Iowa). Married (1) Narcissa Shockley on 3 Sep 1842 (Clinton County, Ohio). He had 2 children with Narcissa. After she died in 1847, George married (2) Sarah A. Botts (1828; 1882) on 2 Apr 1849 (Clinton County, Ohio).

In 1863, George (43) and his brother John (41) were listed in the US Civil War Registration Records, both were living in Des Moines, Iowa, and they were listed as farmers.

George had 10 children with Sarah from 1850 to 1871: *Robert Henry* (1850; 1920), *Cintha Ellen* (1852; 1924), *Thomas Jefferson* (1853; 1921), *Martha Elenore* (1856; 1931), *Lucy Lauina Elwood Coffman* (1858; 1937), *Sarah E.* (1864; 1882), *Joseph William* (1865; 1937), *George Edward* (1868; 1958), *Mary Margaret* (1869; 1934), and *Samuel Duncan* (1871; 1947).

Sarah Ann Botts's sister Cynthia A. Botts (1827; 1860) married George Elwood's brother Hiram William Elwood (1825; 1894) in 1847. Hiram later married Susan Hockette. Hiram died age 60 "a patient at the asylum . . . The remains were sent to friends in Creighton on the 2:20 train."

~~~

Narcissa Shockley

Born ~1822 (Highland, Ohio); died ~1847 at age 25 (Ohio). Married George Elwood on 3 Sep 1842 (Clinton County, Ohio). They had two children. When Narcissa died, she left her spouse and two daughters (ages 3 and 1).

~~~

George and Narcissa Elwood Summary

George Washington Elwood (25) and Narcissa Shockley (18) married in 1842 (Clinton County, Ohio). They had 2 children in 2 years.

1. **Mahala "Hallie" Jane** (25 Jul 1844, Clinton County, Ohio; 23 Mar 1922, Davenport, Iowa) married Edwin Moorman (1835; 1880) on 16 Dec 1862 (Pleasant Plain, Iowa). They had 9 children. See details in Paternal Fourth Generation.

2. **Aleva/Alevia Anna** (13 Jan 1846, Clinton County, Ohio; 1 Mar 1936, Jasper, Iowa; buried Gifford Cemetery, Monroe, Iowa) married John Thompson Woody (1839; 1917) on 11 Mar 1876 (Monroe, Iowa). They had 4 children: **Clyde C.** (1886; 1982), **Arthur E.** (1881; 1970), **George Harmon** (1877; 1940), **Eunice Ethel** (1879; 1964). Aleva died age 90 from a "fall backward while standing" and "infirmities of old age."

> Funeral services for Mrs. John T. Woody, 90, long time resident of Jasper county, will be conducted Wednesday at 1 p.m. from the Methodist Episcopal church in Reasnor. Mrs. Woody died Sunday evening at the home of a step-daughter, Mrs. Ellen Byers, at Reasnor, with whom she had been living for several years. Alevia Ann Elwood was born in Clinton county, Ohio, Jan. 13, 1846, and came with her parents to Jasper county, Ia., when she was a child. The family located southeast of Monroe.
>
> —*The Newton Daily News*, March 3, 1936

The **1856 Iowa Census** lists Washington Elwood and Sarah Elwood living in Des Moines, Iowa, with Mahala J. (12), Aleviann (10), Robert H. (6), Cynthia E. (4), and Thomas J. (2).

The **1860 US Census** lists G. W. Elwood (42) living in Des Moines, Iowa, farmer, with his spouse Sarah (27) and children Mahala G (17), Elleva (15), Robert (10), Cintha E. (Ellen) (8), Thos J. (6), and Louciz (Lucy) (4). Martha was not on list but would have been 5 in this census.

The **1870 US Census** lists Geo W Elwood (50) Warren, Iowa, farmer with his spouse Sarah (43) and children (Cintha) Ellen (17), Thomas (16), Martha (13), Sency (Lucy) (12), Sarah E. (10), Joseph (6), George E. (3), and Mary (1).

The **1880 US Census** lists Sarah (51), Prairie City, Iowa, widowed, "tumor on breast," living with Sarah E (19), Joseph (16), Edward (13), Mary M. (10), and Samuel D. (9).

~~~

**Mahala Jane and sister Aleva: "Grandma Moorman. Leafy Woody, Grandma's full sister. Baby, Harry Moorman."
Circa 1904.**

George and Narcissa's daughter Aleva died age 90. John T. Woody died age 77, Gifford Cemetery, Monroe, Iowa.

Mahala "Hallie" Jane Elwood is the Moorman family ancestor. See details in the Paternal Fourth Generation.

~~~

Summary of Paternal Fourth Generation

Edwin Moorman

Born 25 Oct 1832 (Highland, Ohio); died 13 Aug 1909 at age 76 (Knob Noster, Missouri). Quaker. Buried Knob Noster Cemetery (Knob Noster, Missouri). Edwin was later disowned as a Quaker for marrying out of unity.

My grandfather, Edwin Moorman, was a natural born pioneer. When settlers got too thick around him he sold out and took up another homestead. He was a gunsmith by trade like his father, and was known as one of the best shots in the state of Iowa. He had the finest pack of housed whose voices chorded in the prettiest harmony you ever heard. Grandma Mahala Jane would bake a large pan of cornbread every day for those hounds. Grandpa took his last homestead in Douglas County, Missouri near a small inland town called Vanzant. There on a hundred-sixty acres of rocky land he built a two-room house where he spent the rest of his active life. Then Ernest Moorman, his youngest son, provided a home for both of his parents at Knobnoster, Missouri until their deaths. They are both buried in the cemetery at Knobnoster.

My father [Ellsworth Moorman] was born October 18, 1868 in Bates County near Butler, Missouri. He along with the rest of the Moorman family found the Reorganized Church of Jesus Christ of Latter Day Saints in a very extraordinary way.

Grandpa was out in his gun shop working away when one of the neighbors came I and said, "Ed, did you know that there's a Mormon in town? He's gonna preach in the school house tonight, an' I got twenty men lined up to tar and feather him, and ride him out o' town. We thought you would make a good leader for us."

Gramp said, "I sure will, for we don't want any of those ----- Mormons in this town!"

You see, Grandpa was born in a Quaker family, but had left the Quakers and jointed the Adventist Church. When he became disaffected with it, he had sworn he would never have anything to do with any other church as long as he lived.

They all met outside the school house just before the meeting started, and Grandpa gave them all their instructions. He picked out four of the largest in the gang to take the minister out. The rest were to keep off the crowd till the job was done. Then Grandpa said, "You all know that Solomon says, 'a man is a fool who judges a matter before he hears it'. So when he brings in some of that old Mormon stuff I will stand up. That will be the signal to get him."

BUT Grandpa never did stand up, and strange as it may seem, all but one of those men along with their families joined the church.

A few days afterward the young missionary visited the Moorman home and discovered my father [Ellsworth] had been stone deaf for over two years. Dad was just a kid then. He had lost his hearing from having the Scarlet Fever, and when Brother I. N. White, the young missionary saw him, he asked his parents why they didn't have him administered to.

"We didn't want you to think we were sign seekers," they answered, but he assured them it would be all right. To this they gladly agreed and he proceeded to administer to their son.

The next morning when this young lad awoke he could hear the dishes rattling in the kitchen as his mother was preparing breakfast. He jumped out of bed and ran down the stairs screaming, "I CAN HEAR! I CAN HEAR! I CAN HEAR!"

Dad had the best hearing of any man I ever knew even up to the time of his death. He joined the church in 1880, was called to the office of priest in the after part of his life, and was blessed many times through the ordinances of the church. —From *Wa du ya no bout Us*

Edwin Moorman moved to Jefferson County, Iowa, in 1844. He was baptized a member of the Reorganized Church of Jesus Christ of Latter Day Saints on 24 January 1875 at Polk County, Iowa, by William Nirk. —*Saints' Herald* Obituaries, 1919, p. 912.

Edwin married Mahala "Hallie" Jane Elwood on 16 Dec 1862 (Pleasant Plain, Iowa).

In June 1863, at the age of 30, Edwin registered for the US Civil War draft with his two brothers.

US Civil War Draft Registration, Jun 1863.

US IRS Tax Assessment List, 1862–1918. Edwin Moorman, Patent Rights Deal No. 221. $10.00.

~~~

Mahala "Hallie" Jane Elwood

Mahala Jane Moorman.

Born 25 Jul 1844 (Martinville, Clinton County, Ohio); died 23 Mar 1922 (Davenport, Iowa, at the home of her son John) at age 77, cerebral hemorrhage and uremia. Buried Knob Noster Cemetery (Knob Noster, Missouri). Married Edwin Moorman on 16 Dec 1862 (Pleasant Plain, Iowa).

Mahala Moorman was probably baptized and confirmed in 1875 as a member of the Reorganized Church of Jesus Christ of Latter Day Saints. She received a patriarchal blessing by Patriarch Henry Kemp, in Knob Noster, Missouri, 16 Feb 1908. Copy in possession of editor of this book.

Mahala Jane Elwood Moorman was baptized and confirmed on 25 Nov 1917 as a member of the Church of Jesus Christ of Latter-Day Saints. She was given a patriarchal blessing by Patriarch Hyrum G. Smith, in Salt Lake City, Utah, 15 Oct 1919. Copy in possession of editor of this book.

> Mahala Jane Ellwood . . . lost her own dear mother when only 5 years of age. We children have shed many a tear when she would tell us of her kissing her mother good-bye at bed-time, of her placing one hand upon mother's head, and telling her to take good care of "Little sister" [Alevia] who was 16 months younger, and further adding, "I want you to always be a good girl, so you can meet mother in heaven." How the next morning she came down stairs, to see her father sitting in front of the fireplace, elbow on one knee, head resting in his hand, baby sister in his lap, a white sheet spread across two chairs, how her father took his two motherless little girls by the hand, turned back one corner of the sheet and there lay her dear mother, so cold and white. She asked why she was so cold and he told her, she had gone to heaven. The impression made on mother's mind at this early age, ahd much to do with molding her character, for all through life, her thought was, to so live, that she would be permitted to meet her mother again, and be it said to her credit, that she loved and cherished and competent to give a reason for her faith, and belief. . . . One Sunday morning at church, she told one of her friends that she had accomplished the things, for which she had prayed, and she was ready and willing to go any time. . . . She gently fell asleep, and . . . we could feel the presence of the angels, when they came for her. . . .

—From Neosho M. Jones, *In Memory of Eldora Moorman and Mahala Jane Ellwood*

Ellsworth L. Moorman is the Moorman family ancestor. See details in the Paternal Third Generation.

~~~

Edwin and Hallie Moorman Summary

Edwin (30) married Hallie (18) on 16 Dec 1862 (Pleasant Plain, Iowa). They had 9 children in 23 years.

Edwin and Mahala Jane Moorman, Trenton, Missouri.

Grandfather and Grandmother Moorman, were of the old Pioneer Stock. They were of the Quaker Faith, and Later joined the 7 Day Adventist, but later came in contact with the Reorganized Church of Jesus Christ of Later Day Saints. And was Baptized in 1874 [1875]. Grandfather was a gun smith by trade, also did farming. He loved to roam the woods, and hunt and fish. They were a very happy family, and enjoyed Life. They had many hardships but never complained. Grandpa was an invalid the last Nine years of His life. He and Grandmother are both layed to rest in the Beautiful Knobnoster Mo. Cemetery. The large Headstone at there Grave's, was built by there Son's, Elsworth, and Ernest Moorman. One of there Children (Eugene) is Buried beside them. —From "The Moorman Family"

Left: "Last resting place." Right: Edwin and Mahala Jane Moorman, Knob Noster Cemetery, Missouri, died age 76. Gravestone built by their sons Ellsworth and Ernest Moorman. Their son Eugene is buried beside them.

1. Eldora "Dora" (22 Feb 1864, Pleasant Plain, Iowa; 10 Dec 1922, Salt Lake City, Utah) married Dr. Thomas H. Benton Miller (1839; 1902) on 16 Jan 1886 (Linneus, Missouri). They had 1 child: *Arabelle Jane* (1895; 1977). Died age 58, cystitis. Buried at Salt Lake City Cemetery, Utah.

2. John Winston (15 May 1866, Iowa; 1 Aug 1935, Washington, DC) married (1) Florence Viola Beebe (1870; 1953) in 1887 (Cameron, Missouri). They had 3 children: *Roscoe Francis* (1888; 1942), *Maud M.* (1892; 1895), *Oral* (1894; 1894). Maud died age 3 and Oral died age 5 months. They are buried in a cemetery about six miles north of Cameron, Missouri. Florence and John separated about 1900. John married (2) widow Helena Matzdorf (1869; 1921). After Helena died, John married (3) Eva/Olivia "Strommie" Strom (1878; 1952) on 9 Jul 1923 (Knox, Illinois). John and Ellsworth (brothers) married sisters Florence and Eva. Died age 69. Funeral was held in the Mormon Temple, Washington, DC. Buried Cedar Hill Cemetery, Suitland, Maryland.

3. Ellsworth L. (18 Oct 1868, near Neosho, Bates County, Missouri; 27 Dec 1948, Knob Noster, Missouri) married (1) Eva Estella Beebe (1868; 1937) on 18 Feb 1888 (Cameron, Missouri). They had 6 children. See details in the Paternal Third Generation. After Eva's death, Ellsworth married (2) Minnie "Mickey" Hutchens Scott (1879; 1969) on 3 Mar 1940 (RLDS Church, Knob Noster, Missouri). Died age 80, dropped dead, coronary occlusion, arteriosclerosis. Buried Knob Noster Cemetery, Missouri.

4. Neosho "Sho" C. (7 Feb 1871, Iowa; 3 Jun 1933, Kirksville, Missouri) married (1) Franklin "Frank" Gibson Crouch (1861; 1902) on 9 Jul 1887 (Sullivan, Missouri). They had 3 children: **Kathleen Kate** (1888; 1977), **Alison Dora** (1894; 1912), **Robert Milton** (1896; 1898). After Frank died, married (2) Thomas Henry Jones (1841; 1919) in 1907. Thomas's first wife died in 1906. No children. After Thomas died, married Robert M. Young (1868; 1947) in 1926. No children. Died age 62 from shock after an operation for gallstones. Buried Bethel Cemetery, Kirksville, Missouri.

5. Stella (16 Mar 1874, Des Moines, Iowa; 1 Apr 1941, Kansas City, Missouri) married (1) Judge William R. Frost (?; 1904) on 13 Nov 1893 (Thayer, Missouri). After W. R. Frost died, Stella married (2) William J. Sloan (1867, Canada; 1932) on 8 Jan 1907 (Indiana). William had 3 children from a previous marriage; his wife had died. Married (3) Charles Hines (?; before 1941) in 1932 and lived in Knob Noster, Missouri (divorced about 1935). Died age 67, cerebral thrombosis, pneumonia, hypertension. Buried under the name of Stella Moorman Sloan, Mount Saint Marys Cemetery, Kansas City, Missouri.

6. Maud (2 Nov 1876, Iowa; 1 Jun 1878, Iowa). Died age 1, unknown cause. Buried unknown.

7. Eugene (28 Apr 1879, Polk County, Iowa; 14 Apr 1933, Kansas City, Missouri) married Emma Susan "Patty" Ralls (1885; 1950) on 26 Dec 1905 (Edina, Missouri). Divorced 1914–1918. They had 3 children: **Roma Frances** (1906; 2002), **Robert Keith** (1912; 1913), **Georgia Augustine** (1914; 1990). Died age 53, multiple abscess right lung, emphysema. Buried Knob Noster Cemetery, Missouri.

8. Cumorah "Moley" Missouri birth record has "Savannah Moorman" (5 Jul 1884, Lindley, Missouri; 21 Jan 1929, North Hollywood, California) married John Clinton Chaney (1880; 1958) in 1899 (Drury, Arkansas). They had 2 children: **Mary Belle** (1909; after 1958), **John Clinton Chaney Jr.** (1916; 1919). Died age 44, carcinoma of left breast (for six months) and septicemia (for two months).

9. Ernest James (27 Apr 1887, Lindley, Missouri; 28 Dec 1975, Windsor, Missouri) bricklayer, married Eva May Redfield (1891; 1970) on 18 Dec 1912 (Knob Noster, Missouri). They had 5 children: **Ernestine Harriet** (1913; 1970), **Thyra Jane** (1915; 2011), **Elwood Hendrick** (1916; 1990), **Meleta May** (1925; 2006), **Naomi Louise** (1926; 1985). Died at 88.

~~~

The **1870 US Census** lists "Edmond" farmer and "Jane" living in Richland, Keokuk, Iowa with 3 children: Eldora (6), John (4), and Elsworth (1).

1870 US Census.

The **1880 US Census** lists Ed Moorman and M. Jane living in Palmyra, Warren County, Iowa, with 5 children: John (13), Ellsworth (11), Noesha (9), Stella (6), Eugene (1).

1880 US Census.

The **1930 US Census** lists Ellsworth (61) and Eva (61) living in Johnson County, Missouri.

~~~

Left: Edwin and Hallie's daughter Dora Moorman. Middle: Edwin and Hallie's daughter Dora Moorman Miller, Salt Lake City Cemetery, Utah, died age 58. Right: Dora and her daughter Belle.

Edwin and Hallie's daughter Dora Moorman Miller death certificate.

Left: Edwin and Hallie's daughters Dora and Cumorah. Right: Neosho and Dora Moorman.

Aunt Dora, spent the biggest part of Her Life in Mo. She was Married to Dr. Miller in 1886. They had one Daughter, Arabelle. Dr. Miller only lived 16, Wonderful Years after they were Married. He was considered a very fine Dr. Aunt Dora was a woman of great intelligence. Of vast knowledge. Was also a great Student. She United with the L.D.S. (Morman) Church, in 1915. She was a great Collector of Genealogy, and was a member of the Geneological Society of Utah. Where She lived at the time of Her Death. She did a great deal of Temple work for Her Dead. Every one loved Aunt Dora. She had such a winning Personality, and Happy Laugh. All of Her Family and Friends Loved Her very Dearly. —From "The Moorman Family"

Left: Edwin and Hallie's son John Moorman, 20 years old, 1886. Middle: John and brother Ellsworth. Right: "John Moorman Graduating from Palmer Chiropractor School."

John Moorman and His Bro. Elsworth, Married Sisters. Florence His Wife, and Eva His Brother's. That Made all of the Children double Cousins. We seemed more like Brother and Sister. John was a wonderful Artist. He could Draw and Paint any thing He chose. He was A Chiropractor Dr. in His later Years. He was also a Teacher in the School of Chiropractic, At Daven Port Iowa.   —From "The Moorman Family"

Left: Edwin and Hallie's son Ellsworth Moorman. Middle: 15 years old, 1883. Right: 18 years old, 1886.

Left: Edwin and Hallie's sons, Eugene, Ellsworth, and Ernest. Right: Ellsworth and Ernest.

Elsworth Moorman, Was a brick Layer and Stone Mason, By trade. But like all the Moorman Men, could do almost any thing He wanted to. He and Mother were very fond of hunting, and fishing. They enjoyed Traveling very much. In there Young Married Years, Dad along with His Brother's Worked for the Rail Road. That job took us all over the Country. We were never in one place very long. But it was a happy life, that we all enjoyed. It also gave Mother and Dad A Chance to do lots of Missionary work. For they spread the Gospel, where ever we Went. We moved to Knobnoster Mo. in the year 1905. We had to settle down so us Children could stay in one School for a while. Dad, His Brother's, and Son's Built Silos and other Buildings, over a large area, as far west as Denver. Our evenings at Home, is something to remember. We all enjoyed Singing Hymns and the old songs. Then Mother and Dad would take turns Reading to us. They were both very good readers. And they were always very active Church Members, and us Children always had respect, for our Parent'S. After Mother's Death in 1937. Dad was very lonly. He visited around among His Children, but it wasnt like having a home of His oun. On March 3 rd. 1940. Dad and Minnie Scott were Married. Dads nick name for Her was "Mickey" We all Love Mickey, She made Dad such a good

Wife. Her Husband Died 8 years ago leaving her to rase a large family by Her self. So it was nice for both of them to make a Home once more. Mickey's Hobby was Fishing and Playing the Piano for Her and Dad to sing. Dad also converted Her to the R.L.D.S. Church. Which made them both very happy. They had 8 wonderful years together, but all things must end. On Dec. 17, 1948. Dad droped dead when His time come to go. We were all very proud to call Him Our DAD. And Mickey our second Mother.

—From "The Moorman Family"

Edwin and Hallie's son Ellsworth and spouse Mickey Moorman, 1940.

Left: Edwin and Hallie's daughter Neosho Moorman Jones, 1918, Lucerne, Missouri.
Right: Edwin and Hallie's daughter Neosho Moorman Young, Bethel Cemetery, Kirksville, Missouri, died age 62.

Edwin and Hallie's daughter Neosho Moorman death certificate.

Neosho's daughter **Alison** died age 18, acute gastroenterocolitis and pelvic peritonitis. Neosho's son **Robert** died age 1, cause unknown. Buried Hillside Cemetery, Merrill, Iowa.

Aunt Neosho, was a great lover of Music. She Played the Violin, Piano, and Sang. Also gave Readings, She was a real Entertainer. A wonderful Hostess, Was also a Chiropractor Dr. She was a well Read Woman, could talk on any subject. Aunt Sho was an Excellent Cook, and Gardener, Her Flower garden's were Beautiful, Like Her Life. And Personality. Aunt Sho was always doing something for those in need. Her first Husband, Frank Crouch Died when Her Children were quite young, Kate only 14, and Alison 8, She did Nurseing, and Entertaining to support them. 5, years later She Met and Married Uncle Tom Jones. He had a Beautiful Home, called "Oak Hill" aunt Sho and the Girls made it a real Home. Uncle Tom, raised Throughbred Horse's, and made all the big Horse Shows. He always took Aunt Sho with Him. They had a wonderful like togather. He also played the Violin, they had loads of friends and did lots of Entertaining.

Kate and Alison were both very find Pianist's. and Uncle Tom was very proud to call them His Daughter's. Kate was Married to Clyde Myers about two years after Aunt Sho and Uncle Tom were Married. When Malcolm was Born He was the "Pearl of great price" to Aunt Sho. Her First Grang-child to live. She predicted Great things for Him, that have come true. For Malcolm is now a Wonderful Artist. I spent two Months with Aunt Sho and Uncle Tom in 1918. While Roy was serving in the Army. Grand-mother Moorman was there also, and we all had such a nice time togather. Aunt Sho and I, did quite a bit of Entertaining. We helped to take care of sick folk's thet couldn't to hire some one. But we both enjoyer doing what we could. I never saw Uncle Tom again after I left there. He Died the next year 1919. That left Aunt Sho alone once more. But they had 12, Wonderful years togather. Six years later, Aunt Sho Married Robert Young, and went to live on the farm in Mercer Mo. She lived 10, years there, He had a nice Home, and with all of Her lovely Furniture in it. She made it a real Home for Uncle Bob and His Sister that had always lived there. Aunt Show had such lovely flowers. And they were there prettiest when She Died. And we made many Beautiful Floral Sprays and Wreath's, from Her oun Flowers, for Her Funeral.

—From "The Moorman Family"

Neosho Moorman Jones.

Edwin and Hallie's granddaughter Kate and spouse Clyde Myers, Wichita, Kansas.

VISITING IN WICHITA—Mr. and Mrs. Malcolm Myers, former residents, respectively, of Wichita and Conway Springs, are visiting their parents while Myers' paintings and prints are on exhibit at the Wichita Art Museum. They have been in Mexico City and are returning to Minneapolis, where Myers is a professor of art at the University of Minnesota.—(Eagle Staff Photo.)

MALCOLM MYERS, Professor of Art at the University of Minnesota, will have a one-man show in the Minnesota Gallery in May and June. Born in Missouri, Myers received his Bachelor of Arts degree at the University of Wichita, and a Master of Arts degree at the State University of Iowa in 1940, studying under Emil Ganso. After the war, he returned to Iowa, and received a Master of Fine Arts degree in 1946, working with Mauricio Lasansky. He taught printmaking at the State University of Iowa for two years before coming to Minnesota in 1948.

Myers has exhibited in every national print show for many years, among them Philadelphia, Seattle, Chicago, New York, Cincinnati, Wichita, and Baltimore. His print *Saint Anthony*, in the Walker Art Center collection, was selected as one of the "100 Best Prints of the Year" in 1946, and is also in the collection of the Library of Congress. He works in all techniques of the graphic art: woodcut, etching, engraving, lithography, drypoint, aquatint, and monoprint. He also paints in oil, gouache, and watercolor. Two of his oils were selected for the Minnesota Gallery show VISITORS FROM MINNESOTA which went to Nebraska recently. In his teaching and in his work Myers advocates an open mind and free experimentation with techniques. The resulting plates are full of rich variety and a controlled use of technical effects for purposes of expression. A selection will be for sale.

Edwin and Hallie's great-grandson Malcolm Myers.

Left: Edwin and Hallie's daughter Stella (right) with Hallie.
Right: Stella, Cumorah, Eugene, Edwin, Ernest, and Mahala Jane Moorman, Harris, Missouri.

Left: Edwin and Hallie's daughter Stella Moorman, Mountain Grove, Missouri, 19 years old, 1893.
Middle: Stella Moorman and W. R. Frost. Right: Stella Moorman with unknown men.

In **1910**, Edwin and Hallie's daughter Stella lived in Chicago, Illinois, with William Sloan and his 3 children from a previous marriage. In **1920**, Stella lived in Natrona, Wyoming, with William. In **1930**, Stella lived in Boone County, Arkansas, with William. In **1940**, Stella lived in Kansas City, Missouri.

Stella's first Marriage. W. R. Frost Nov. 13, 1898. At Thayer Mo. Oreg. Co. He only leved a few years, But they were very happy years. Then Aunt Stella was left a young Widow. Later, She took A job caring for Three Motherless Children. In the W. J. Sloan Home. Aunt Stella loved Children, but never had any of her oun. The Sloan Children, Lucy, Bertha, and George, soon come to love Her like they did there "Dead" mother. In about the year 1907. Stella Frost, was Married to the Childrens Father, William J. Sloan. He was a Manager of one of Chicagoes large Department Stores. They had a nice Home, and Aunt Stella was Very Happy, for she loved the Children like they were her very oun. And they did her. She raised them to be 3 of the finest Children. They all Married Good Companions. After all the Children were Married, Aunt Stella and Uncle Will, came west to live, First to Casper Wyo. Then later, to Ark. Where they spent the rest of there life till his Death. He was Buried there in Bellfonte Ark. I think he Died in 1932. Stella Sloan, then Married Charley Hines. And lived at Knobnoster MO. This Marriage ended in a Divorce in about 1935. Later she entered "The Little Sisters Of The Poor" and lived there till her Death, April 1, 1941.

—From "The Moorman Family"

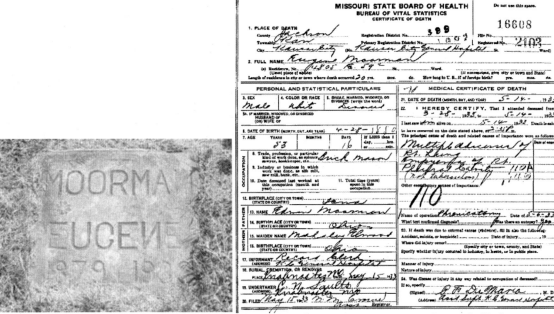

Left: Edwin and Hallie's son Eugene Moorman, Knob Noster Cemetery, Missouri, died age 53.
Right: Eugene Moorman death certificate.

Eugene's daughter **Roma** married Cecil Dale Beebe (1901; 1996) in 1924 (Kansas City, Missouri). Cecil was the son of Myron Francis Beebe and Laura Dale Morrison. Eugene's son **Robert Keith** died 9 months old of lobular pneumonia. He's buried in Mount McCaleb Cemetery in Mackay, Idaho.

Left: Edwin and Hallie's granddaughter Eugene's daughter Augustine Moorman Werbe and son.
Middle: Edwin and Hallie's grandchildren Mary Belle and John Chaney.
Right: Edwin and Hallie's daughter Cumorah Moorman Chaney, Forest Lawn Memorial Park, Glendale, California, died age 44.

Uncle Eugene and Aunt Emma were Divorced after 15, years or more, Aunt Emma Married Raymond Fuller, and had one Son Billie, so Roma and Augustine have a half Brother that they both adore. And he is a wonderful Man. Uncle Gene never Married again. Every one loved Uncle Gene. He was a Master Brick Layer, had worked on the largest Bldg's in N.Y. and other places. He was a great lover of out door life. Hunting, Fishing, and Swimming. It seemed a tragedy, to the entire family, when he died so young only 54. He was a wonderful Father, Brother, and Uncle, that we missed very much.

—From "The Moorman Family"

We all called Aunt Comorah, "Moley." She and Uncle John lived in K.C.K. many years. He was an Electrician, and has His own Electric Shop. Aunt Moley worked for a long time as a Cashier at the Old "Electric Park," in K.C. Mo. They were Married-9-years before Mary-Belle was Born, So She was a very Precious Child, The Pride and Joy of there Life. Then 7, years later Little John was Born. He only lived 2, years. Not long after Little John's Death, they Moved to Calif. And Settled there. Uncle John worked at one of the Hollywood Movie Studio's, as there Chief Electrician.   —From "The Moorman Family"

Left: Edwin and Hallie's son Ernest Moorman, 1967. Middle: Windsor, Missouri, 1970. Right: Eva May and Ernest.

Left: Elwood Moorman (on left) with Ernest Moorman (on right). Right: Ernest Moorman.

ERNEST MOORMAN

Ernest Moorman, 89, Windsor, Mo., formerly of Independence, died Sunday at a nursing home in Clinton, Mo. He was born in Lindley, Mo., and lived in Independence 34 years before moving to Windsor in 1960. Mr. Moorman was a bricklayer 50 years before he retired. He was a member of the Reorganized Church of Jesus Christ of Latter Day Saints, Independence. He leaves a son, Elwood Moorman, 8806 E. 9th; three daughters, Mrs. Thyra Heater, Calhoun, Mo., and Mrs. Naomi Midkiff, 1517 Geronimo, and Mrs. Meleta Baker, 18203 Hanthorn, both of Independence; 13 grandchildren, and 20 great-grandchildren. Services will be at 1:30 p.m. Tuesday at the Hadley Chapel, Windsor; burial in the Knob Noster, Mo., Cemetery. Friends may call from 7 to 8:30 o'clock tonight at the chapel.

SERVICES FOR

ERNEST MOORMAN

April 27, 1886   December 28, 1975

will be held at the
HADLEY FUNERAL HOME
Tuesday, December 30, 1975   1:30 p.m.

INTERMENT
Knob Noster Cemetery
Knob Noster, Missouri

SERVICES CONDUCTED BY
Elder Barney Fuller

CASKET BEARERS
Rex Cook   Dennis Ray Midkiff
Eugene Baker   Gary Baker
Richard Midkiff   Ernest Moorman

ARRANGEMENTS BY
HADLEY FUNERAL HOME
Windsor, Missouri

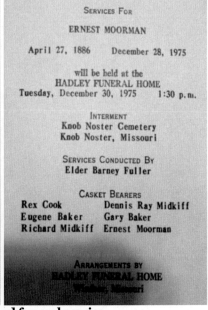

Ernest Moorman obituary and funeral service.

Left: Edwin and Hallie's grandson, Elwood Moorman. Right: Elwood and his wife.

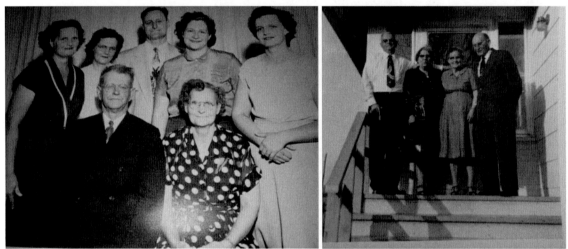

Left: Edwin and Hallie's son Ernest and Eva May (seated in front). Top: Earnestine (Mickey), Thyra, Elwood, Meleta, Naomi. 20 Jun 1953. Right: Ernest Moorman, Ella Wood, Eva May Moorman, Erwin Moorman.

Summary of Paternal Third Generation

Ellsworth L. Moorman

Born 18 Oct 1868 (Butler, Bates County, Missouri); died 27 Dec 1948 of a sudden coronary occlusion and arteriosclerosis at age 80 (Knob Noster, Missouri). Buried at Knob Noster Cemetery (Knob Noster, Missouri). Married Eva Beebe in 1888 (Cameron, Missouri). After Eva died in 1937, he married Minnie "Mickey" Scott (1879; 1969) in 1940 (Knob Noster, Missouri).

See additional information about Ellsworth under Edwin Moorman from *Wa du ya no bout Us*.

Eva Beebe Moorman's details are given under "Maternal Moorman Family." The children of Eva and Ellsworth are listed after this information in the "Summary of Maternal/Paternal Second Generation."

Left: Ellsworth Moorman. Right: Erwin, Oscar, Ellsworth holding Ella.

**Left: Elsworth and Erwin Moorman. Middle: Ellsworth and granddaughters Helen, Thelma, and Alta June.
Right: Ellsworth and granddaughter Virginia.**

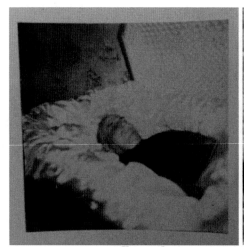

Ellsworth Moorman, Knob Noster Cemetery, died age 80.

FILED JAN 10 1949

THE DIVISION OF HEALTH OF MISSOURI
STANDARD CERTIFICATE OF DEATH

40592

Ellsworth Moorman death certificate, died age 80.

~ ~ ~

Ellsworth and Eva Moorman Summary

Ellsworth (19) married Eva (19) in 1888 (Cameron, Missouri). They had 6 children in 18 years.

My father, Elsworth Moorman, was united with my mother, Eva Beebe in marriage at Cameron, Missouri February 18, 1888.

Dad was a steam engineer for locomotives, steam shovels, and many other kinds of engines. This kept our family on the move from place to place until I was about twelve years old. We then settled down in Knobnoster, Missouri.

Mother was a natural born missionary woman. She loved the gospel and the church very much, and whenever it was possible she had the missionaries come to our place and hold a series of meetings. One of these wonderful experiences took place near St. Louis, Missouri where Dad had taken a job of steam shoveling. There they would be burning clay to make ballast for the railroads, and the job would last at least six months.

The night before we boarded the train to join Dad Mother had a dream in which she saw the place where we were to live. She saw a small school house about a mile away in which she was teaching pupils ranging in age from childhood to grown ups. When we got off the train the next day mother exclaimed, "I have seen all this place in my dream, and there is the school house where I am going to teach."

The next Sunday after we moved in, Mother dressed up her three children, my older brother Oscar, my younger sister Ella, and me and took us to Sunday School. We were welcomed with open arms, and mother was asked to teach a Young Adult class. She accepted the offer and soon had the confidence of the whole class. For the next Sunday she asked them to bring their bibles. That day she hurried through their Universal quarterly lesson and then started in on the first principles of the Gospel, faith, repentance, laying on of hands, etc.

About the fifth Sunday mother became aware that all the rest of the Sunday School had become very quiet. She hastily excused herself for going overtime, but the president of the Sunday School said, "Go on, Sister. We have never heard anything like what you are teaching before, and we want to hear more."

So it was that before long a missionary series had been arranged, and after heating the gospel message preached by two elders who came for the following three weeks, almost all of the congregation there accepted the gospel and became Latter Day Saints.

It was at this place that mother had a very bad accident. The horse she was driving was frightened and ran away with her and us children in the buggy. The buggy overturned throwing us all out on the ground. It was demolished, and mother's ankle was crushed. She was taken to a hospital in St. Louis, and two of our elders came and administered to her. One of them spoke to her under the power of the Holy Spirit and told her that she would not have any pain when the doctors would set the bones in her ankle. However, she was told that she would not be healed right away. This prediction was fulfilled just as they said. Then three years later she was visited by an angelic personage who administered to her in the night. He told her then that she could throw away her crutches, for she would never need them again; and she didn't. But she always had a limp after that until the day of her death, October 17, 1937.   —From *Wa du ya no bout Us*

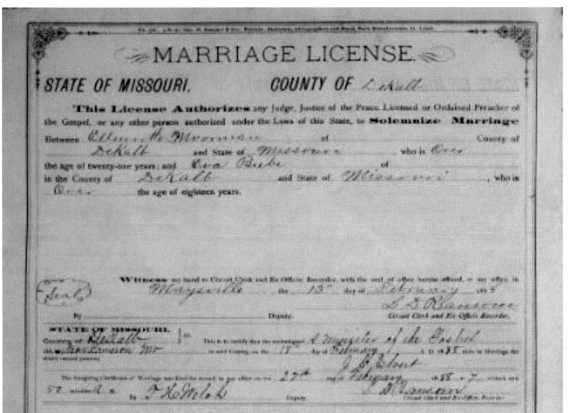

Ellsworth Moorman and Eva Beebe marriage license, DeKalb County, Missouri, 18 Feb 1888.

Ellsworth and Eva Beebe Moorman, Osceola, Iowa.

~~~

Florence Moorman Guy

The Moorman Home in Knob Noster, MO

Left: Moorman baptism. Right: Moorman Home, Knob Noster, Missouri.

Back row: Florence, Erwin, Harry, Eva, Elsworth
Front row: Roy, Ella, Ethel, Oscar, Gela

OSCAR   EL   ERWIN   HARR
FLORENCE   GRANDMOTHER   E

RLDS Church built by the Moorman boys

Florence's painting of Christ
it was painted for the Knob Noster
R.L.D.S. Church that the Moorman
boys built.

Left: back row: Laura Beebe, Ellsworth Moorman, Oscar Moorman, Enid Wanbaugh.
Front row: David Moorman and Steve Wanbaugh. Right: Ella, Ellsworth, Mickey, and Florence.

Right: Eva E. and Ellsworth Moorman, Knobnoster Cemetery, Missouri.

Upper L- Dad Moorman and his
5 Children Just 2,weeks before His Death.Next The Family
at K.N.1913.Next,Family at K.
N.1928.or 1929. Ella&Erwin.
Top R,Family,Oscar Erwin,Ella
1907.at K.N.Bottom R,Ella,
Oscar and Erwin about 1900.

~~~

Unable to locate the family in the **1890 US Census.** Most of these records were destroyed in a fire at the Commerce Department Building in January 1921.

Unable to locate any family members in the **1900 US Census.** Ellsworth and Eva's son William Oral was born in 1899 (unknown location) and died in 1900. He is buried in Murray, Iowa.

In the **1910 US Census,** E. L. (42) and Eva (41) are living in Washington, Missouri, with Oscar (21), Irwin (18), Ella (16), Harry (6), Florence (2). Eva is listed as a photographer. E. L. and both sons are listed as masons in the concrete industry.

In the **1920 US Census,** E. L. (51) and Eva Mormon (51) are living in Washington, Missouri, with son Harry (15) and daughter Florence (12). E. L. is listed as a mason in the brick industry. Harry is listed as a mason apprentice. The women are listed as "none."

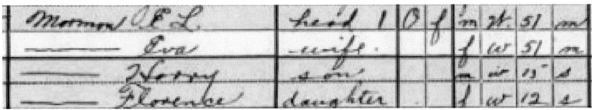

1920 US Census.

In the **1930 US Census,** Ellsworth (61) and Eva Moorman (61) are living in Washington, Missouri. Ellsworth is listed as a laborer in the brick mason industry.

1930 US Census.

~~~

Oscar Myron Moorman is the Moorman family ancestor. See details in the Paternal Second Generation.

~~~

Moorman Silos

Moorman Silos
1920's

Above EE Moorman & Ralph Woolsey

Top: Ernest Moorman
Below: Helen, Florence & Ella

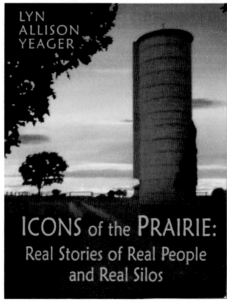

The Moormans and Their Tileglyphic Art

This was a family of boys whose names began with the letter E—all except one, Oscar. Here they are: Edwin, Ellsworth, Erwin, Oscar, Ernest, another Ernest, and Eugene. Just a bit confusing, isn't it? Maybe a genealogical chart will help: (3 generations)

1) Edwin
   2) Ellsworth
      3) Erwin (a real joker)
      3) Oscar (how he got the 'O' I do not know)
      3) Ernest
   2) Ernest (Ernie) (188T-1975)
      3) Eugene

There were, of course, names of mothers, daughters, cousins and aunts but the 'E' pattern did not apply to them.

Mildred Moorman Kester in Independence, Missouri, was kind in giving me the Moorman family information. Mildred's father was Erwin, the son of Ellsworth who had taught his son Erwin the art of bricklaying.

Ellsworth

Ellsworth, son of Edwin, lived in Knob Noster, Missouri. There he built for himself a storm cellar behind his house. It became so admired that he received orders from other people in town. So his reputation as a bricklayer was established.

Ellsworth is buried in the Knob Noster Cemetery and his tombstone is unique—a   brick fireplace shape. For some time a long, plastic box rested on the

Yeager

Moorman Tombstone

grass in front of the fireplace. The strange, sarcophagus-shaped box often held artificial flowers. It was removed some seven years ago. The memorial fireplace tombstone remains

~147~

with worn, chipped, loose bricks. It is a large but sad reminder of a brickmason who, maybe wishes someone to repair it, or who, maybe, just laughs because the men of his family are known to love jokes.

Erwin

Erwin Moorman worked for a Kansas City brick company part of the time. One of his independent endeavors was in Elk City, Kansas, and his family went with him. Before they started, Erwin purchased a car from a friend for payments of ten dollars a month. Erwin did not wish to drive so the friend drove the car to Elk City for him. At the silo building location the family set up camp, a tent, and some rough furniture which they made of the wood from trees in nearby groves. The children really enjoyed their new, wild life. They played in the woods, waded in the crystal-clear, cool water of a nearby creek, fished, ate outdoors, played and napped on the shaded grass.

One day while Erwin was hard at work in the developing silo, the thirty foot tall center pole fell and injured him. His wife, Ethel, tried to help him; she stumbled and broke a toe. Still concerned about her husband, she insisted that he must see a doctor. Erwin recommended the same for her. Finally they did walk into town to a doctor's and then walked back. Why they walked no one now seems to know. Maybe Erwin was afraid to try to drive the car; maybe it was out of gas, maybe there was no "filling station" out in that rough, rural area, but other working men were, no doubt, ordered to keep on working!

This event carried Erwin to his decision to retire and move to Independence. There he built a Spanish style house at 825 South Wesley Street very near a spring, for there was no indoor plumbing in the house. Their home was unique with arched, stone-framed windows and singular, outdoor stone arches for decorations.

Ernest, Tileglyphic Artist

Ernest (Ernie) Moorman, brother of Ellsworth was born April 27, 1886 in Lindley, Missouri. He married Eva May Redfield in 1912 in Knob Noster. His brother taught him masonry, and this became Ernest's life work. Ernest was unusual and interested in everything. He wrote poetry, long, rhyming verse of the style taught in school in his time. Of his profession-type work he wrote:

> Bricklayers are a bunch of men
> you find in every city.
> You see them working now and then
> when the weather's nice and pretty.
> They bow their heads and bend their backs
> without ever lookin' 'round.
> For eight long hours it never slacks,
> just spread and paste 'em down.

Also, of those working men he said,

> And right here I am telling you that I'd
> sure like to be
> With those bricklayers tried and true;
> they're good enough for me.

In all his poetry he never mentioned tile silos, just bricks.

Of bricklayers he wrote,

> … he travels here and there
> where he thinks best…
> but there is always something wrong
> … he quits and moves along
> … the waterboy was lazy…
> the whole … bunch was crazy.

A familiar command to the workers was "Be sure you slush the wall." (slushing meant washing the interior walls of silos to remove loose bits of mortar and finally to paint the walls with a sealing, protective liquid.)

Ernest also wrote,

> Yes, I know I've said a lot
> about those boys that isn't so.
> There are a few without a doubt, and some
> perhaps you know,
> But most of them are splendid men
> who like the building trade,
> A trade that dates away back
> when old Babel's tower was made.

~149~

Lyn Allison Yeager

One silo builder, of the Moormans, (maybe Ernest) constructed a silo on a farm now owned by Raymond ("Bud") Wasson on a rural route near Knob Noster. On that farm is also a Radcliff silo which has white painted slabs around the top edge. Raymond bought this farm in 1948. In 1914 there had been a wooden silo on the farm. Then a tile silo, struck by lightning in 1940, was rebuilt by a "Sedalia bricklayer" who engraved on the inside these words, "This silo was built to last forever and a year more." This same statement has been seen in at least one other silo of the area but no one swears to the author's name. Well, Sedalia is near Knob Noster and Ernest was always joking. So—it might have been his work. Now water stands in this roofless, forsaken silo and present time is part of "forever." Once, a cow drank seepage from this silo and became slightly tipsy. Had Ernest Moorman been there he would no doubt have laughed heartily and probably would have written a poem about a drunk cow.

In a box of family pictures was one created from two others. Some humorous family member had cut Ernest's head from one snapshot and pasted it onto the top of a silo in another snapshot. The joke-creation shows Ernest smiling a big, fun-filled grin. His relatives' understood and easily accepted Ernest's lifetime occupation and the joy he showed in everything he did.

Perhaps Ernest Moorman was Missouri's (and maybe the United States') first tileglyphic artist.

Walter Stephenson

In August of 1919 a red tile silo was reported built by "a stonemason from Knob Noster." This is just outside town on the farm of Mr. and Mrs. Sammy Lane. Time, and once a touch of lightning, had worn some of the concrete from between tiles. When I went to this silo, I crawled inside but found a floor covered with wet, soft mud. I drove to the Knob Noster lumber yard and purchased some wide, flat sideboards and placed them on the mud so I could stand and inspect the silo's inside walls. There I was amazed at what I found. Carved into the tiles and caulking was the large, nude figure of a man running and yelling "Help!" He was being chased by a panther type animal.

I asked the owners about the carvings but they knew nothing. Then in town I inquired

Silo of Tileglyphic Art, inside

~150~

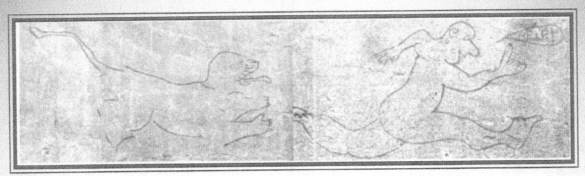

Photo by Bruce Matthews, Photographer - Kansas City, MO.

and asked the business men, people in the library, my friends and acquaintances. No one could explain. The majority didn't even know the picture was in the silo but most seemed to remember the silo builder to be Ernest Moorman.

So I began my research and learned of the history of an ancient art of rock engraving. The word styleglyph means "... a picture cut into a surface or carved in relief." Next I learned that in the C6a Valley in northeastern Portugal, where a huge government dam was to be constructed, drawings were found on rock cliffs. The dam construction was halted. Now UNESCO declares this place "a permanent archeological park." The engraved pictures include "a horse with its head turned in two directions, an ibex looking backward and forward, fish, and three large, superimposed aurocks measuring almost six feet tall, plus the only Paleolithic human figure from this area." These were *called petroglyphs* because they were on rock cliffs. *Petro* means rock. Archeology and history professors have combined research to determine those ancient artists' reasons for creating such pictures and have presented the theory that "animals' heads and forequarters in multiple positions ... indicate movement," and that those primitive people knew movement even as children and adults have always done. Some human need seems to be satisfied in those glyphs. Modern Ernest Moorman did not copy those petroglyphs. He died before they were found, but he would have been interested had he known.

I now understand how the tileglyphs which I've found and named (in Missouri) might have satisfied their maker's need but what was that need or purpose?

I began my search in Knob Noster and discovered there was a Panther Street and a Panther Creek, and these gave me an idea. I went to the town High School office and asked if the school had ever had students named Moorman. The answer was, "Yes, a long time ago."

Then I asked, "Were any of them on the school's athletic teams?"

"We don't know and those old records were destroyed by a fire."

Then I said, "What is the school sports' animal emblem?"

The quick response, "Panther."

That reply seems to suggest a source for the origin of the tileglyph in the silo. Perhaps the builder was a town citizen who liked the panther emblem because he had a son, or other relative, who was in the school's sports. Maybe he was a town resident proud of the Knob Noster teams. Either would have been reasonable. Anyway it is not a common silo engraving. It is unusual and original and created by someone for his own reasons. Maybe the artist was Ernest Moorman.

Graffiti and Architectural Cousins

The word *graffito* means a drawing or inscription made on a wall or other surface, usually in a place easily seen by the public. The plural of the word *is graffiti*. These are drawings or engravings, maybe not artistic, but expressions of anger or rebellion against others more fortunate than their inscribers.

As early as 1650 graffiti were scratched and scribbled on walls in Europe, often on lovely glazed tiles. So, again, United States ghettos' graffiti scratchers should learn there is "nothing new under the sun," not even graffiti!

In the year 2000 the mayor of Paris, France announced that the city had a new program to clean all buildings which were disfigured by forms of graffiti. The city had about forty percent of some ninety thousand buildings so defaced. The cost was estimated at seventy-two million dollars.

Sometimes graffiti may be artistic and in the 21st century were recognized, featured in newspapers, magazines and TV. In a way, graffito is a descendant of cave dwellers' petroglyphic art. Today it is sometimes evil, sexual, physical, picturesque, even including hieroglyphic showing letters, sounds and writing.

In the United States, silo builders often engraved those circular, enduring grain bins with names and dates. Public buildings had "corner stones" enclosing historical items or records and the stones were engraved with names and dates.

Silos, granaries, homes, churches, public buildings and highways are all worthy parts of man's historical relationships and naive pride in accomplishment.

Near Warrensburg, Missouri, south off, but near Highway 50, stand three old silos of different colors. They are near an antique barn built without nails but with wooden pegs.

So we have still with us today silos, towers, brick walls, buildings, and corner stones holding graffiti.

Summary of Maternal/Paternal Second Generation

Ellsworth and Eva Moorman had 6 children.

Oscar Myron Moorman

Born 26 Apr 1889 (Cameron, Missouri) Friday at 9:30 A.M. He weighed 8 pounds, 10 ounces. Died 18 Nov 1963 at age 74 (Kansas City, Missouri). Buried at Knob Noster Cemetery (Knob Noster, Missouri). Married Gela Lela Cook (1893; 1972) on 5 Jun 1918 (1028 West Maple Avenue, Independence, Missouri). They had 4 children: *Virginia Merle* (1920; 1997), *Enid Louise* (1921; 2003), *Eleanor Rose "Mickey"* (1928; 1987), *David Kent* (1946; 1975) adopted April 1946.

Oscar and Gela have a Family to be Proud of. Oscar's Hobby is "Music." He has played With Many Bands. He has Travled all over the Co. With the American Legion Band. Playing for State and National Conventions. He also plays the Saw. Enjoys Hunting, Fishing, and Boating. They have a nice Cabin at the Lake of the Ozarks, that all of there Family, and Friends enjoy. All of the Moorman Family enjoy, out-door Sport's. —From "The Moorman Family"

Erwin Everett Moorman

Born 31 Mar 1892 (Cameron, Missouri) Thursday at 8:00 P.M. He weighed 10 pounds. Died 30 Jun 1990 at age 98 (Independence, Missouri). Buried in Mound Grove Cemetery (Independence, Missouri). Married Ethel Leona Hawley (1893; 1986) on 15 Dec 1912 (RLDS Church, Knob Noster, Missouri). They had 4 children: *Helen Loduska* (1913; 1999), *Thelma Louise* (1914; 2011), *Alta June* (1916; 1971), *Melba Geraldine* (1918; 2011).

All of the Erwins Daughters, and there Children are Musicians, and all Sing. Music was a part of Erwin and Ethel's life, and all of the Children were Raised on it, and working in the church. And all of there Children and Grandchildren, that are old enough, belong to the Church. Erwin and Ethel's hobby, have been helping people. Both in Material things, and Spiritual things. There Family shows what a good pattern, was set before them. They are all happy families in the Church togather. —From "The Moorman Family

Ella Neosho Moorman Wood

Born 5 Mar 1895 (Cameron, Missouri) Monday at 10:30 P.M. She weighed 9.5 pounds. Died 28 Mar 1966 at age 72 (Kansas City, Missouri). Buried at Knob Noster Cemetery (Knob Noster, Missouri). Married Roy August Wood (1891; 1956) on 23 Dec 1912 (minister's home, Knob Noster, Missouri). No children.

Roy and Ella Had no Children. Roy was a Barber By Trade. Always owning his oun shop Ella was a Beauty Operator, had a "Shoppe" in Kansas City Kan. Many years. After Selling out, about the Year 1938. She started doing Volunteer Red Cross work First doing "Gray Lady" Work at Bethany Hospital. Teaching First Aid and Accident Prevention, Classes, Also doing Entertaining, at Wadsworth Veteran Hospital Now for over 16, Years. And still on the job. Roy and Ella traveled a great deal. As long as there Parents lived, they took them on long trips, which they all enjoyed a lot. Roy and Elle, Traveled all over the Co. with the American Legion Band. Roy was a Trombone player, and Ella was the Song Leader, for the Clown Band, also took care of all of the First Aid, and carried our Medical Supplies. The last 2, years of Roy's life was spent in the Hospital, and at Home. Roy's Hobby was Music, Ella has several Hobbies, Stamp Collecting, Making Records, Music, and Making Family Records, and Traveling, all over the Co. —From "The Moorman Family"

William Oral Moorman

Born 7 Oct 1899 (Osceola, Iowa) Saturday 9:00 P.M. He weighed 10 pounds. Died 29 Dec 1900 (Murray, Iowa) at age 1. "He strangled and evidently burst an artery in his lungs." Buried Murray Cemetery (Murray, Iowa). On gravestone is engraved "son of EL & EE, aged 1 yr."

Harry Ellsworth Moorman

Born 19 Feb 1904 (Laredo, Missouri) Friday at 6:00 A.M. He weighed 11 pounds. Died 24 Mar 1962 at age 58 (Brooklyn, New York). Buried Knob Noster Cemetery (Knob Noster, Missouri). Married Kathryn Griffith Davis Healey (1915; 2005) on 16 Oct 1935 (RLDS Church, Brooklyn, New York). They had 1 child: *Sandra Kay* (1939; after 2021).

Harry and Kay, have lived all of there Married life at the same Address, 9701, Shore Road, Brooklyn-9-N.Y. Harry worked for the Federal Reserve Bank in N. Y. City for 20 years. But for the past 10 or 12 years

He had been in the Import and Export Business. Since Sandra is grown, and attending College, Kay also works. Harry's work keeps him traveling on the road most of the time. I think Harry and Kay's Hobby is work. For they seem to keep busy all the time. —From "The Moorman Family"

Florence Geneva Moorman Guy

Born 29 Nov 1907 (Knob Noster, Missouri) Friday at 7:00 P.M. She weighed 10 pounds. Died 2 Aug 2003 at age 95 (Bow, Washington). Buried at Bay View Cemetery (Mount Vernon, Washington). Married John "Jack" Edward Guy (1904; 2004) on 5 Sep 1933 (RLDS Church, Kansas City, Kansas). They had 3 children: **Ed** (1934; after 2021), **Pat** (1936; after 2021), **Eva** (1950; after 2021).

Jack Guy works for T.W.A. Air Lines, so he and the family have traveled a great deal. While there Children were growing up. Florence is also an Artist, Paints wonderful Pictures. Plays the Saw, and is an excellent Cook. Jack is a Master Machinac, and can fix anything. They are all good Travelers, and enjoy Traveling. They have a family to be Proud of. —From "The Moorman Family"

~~~

Oscar Moorman

1920 US Census, 1502 W. Walnut, Independence, Missouri.

Oscar M. Moorman, head, male, 30, born 1890, Missouri, married, white, father born Missouri, mother born Iowa, bricklayer, house.

Gela C. Moorman, female, 26, born 1894, Tennessee, married, white, wife, father born Virginia, mother born Tennessee, no profession.

Lila B. Andes, female, 24, born 1896, Missouri, widowed, white, boarder, school teacher

Virginia Budd, female, 20, born 1900, Missouri, single, white, boarder, stenographer, public office

Oscar Myron Moorman.

Left: Second row, left to right: Oscar and Erwin Moorman. Right: Erwin, Ella, Roscoe, Oscar.

THE SERVICE MAN

WHAT HE IS—AND WHAT HE DOES FOR YOU.

What our factory superintendent is to our factory, he is to our buyers. He is the man who superintends the making of American Tile Silos, not in the factory, but on the farm.

He's the man who knows silo building—not from theory, but from experience. For instance, one Service Man, Mr. Oscar Moorman, has built with his own hands over 125 Silos. He is an expert mason, but he has graduated from that class.

His business now is to show new masons HOW it's done.

He travels through the country from Silo to Silo and should your mason not be familiar with Silo construction, he stays a day with him and gets him started.

This saves us sending out masons, and still puts an expert on every job.

Incidentally, he sometimes writes an order or two. No, he is not a salesman—far from it—but he is in a position to know facts at first hand, and that's what a prospective customer wants, for if he knows the real facts he is sure to decide in favor of the American Tile Silo.

Last of all, he is a pleasant man to do business with and thoroughly familiar with his work, which he goes about cheerfully.

This is only a part of our service, but it is a typical example to show you how willing we are to do anything which will convenience our customers.

We are not through with an American Tile Silo until it is erected and ready to fill.

OSCAR MOORMAN, SERVICE MAN

Pamphlet by the American Tile Silo Company, featuring Oscar Moorman as "The Service Man."

 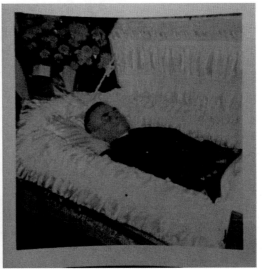

Oscar Myron Moorman.

OSCAR M. MOORMAN

Oscar M. Moorman, 74, Knob Noster, Mo., died today at the Veterans Administration hospital. He was born in Cameron, Mo., and lived in Independence 25 years before moving to Knob Noster five years ago. He was a retired brickmason. He was a member of the Reorganized Latter Day Saints church in Knob Noster. He was a veteran of World War I. He was a member of the Tirey J. Ford American Legion post in Independence, the 40 & 8 society, the American Legion guard of honor, was a member of the Greater Kansas City American Legion band many years. He leaves his wife, Mrs. Gela C. Moorman of the home; three daughters, Mrs. Virginia Zukowsky, 1028 West Maple, Independence, Mrs. Enid Cruce, 13401 Kemper drive, Independence, and Mrs. Eleanor Sartwell, 2415 South Sterling, Independence; a son, David K. Moorman, Hermosa Beach, Calif.; two sisters, Mrs. Ella Wood, 826 Tauromee, Kansas City, Kansas, and Mrs. Florence Guy, Kennydale, Wash.; a brother, Erwin Moorman, Lamoni, Ia., and nine grandchildren. Funeral services will be at 1:30 o'clock Wednesday at the Speaks chapel. Burial will be in Knob Noster cemetery. Friends may call from 7 to 9 o'clock Tuesday night at the chapel.

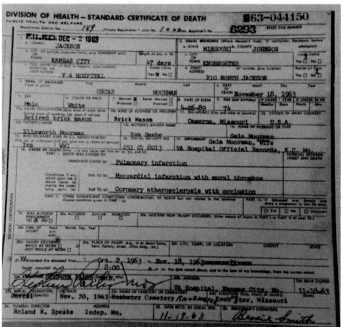

Post Cards to Oscar Moorman, 1913–1952

Front: Haf Youse Forgotten Your Friendts in Independence If Not, Vy Don't Youse Rite

Postmark: 1. Independence, MO, April 19, 1913, 12 M. 2. Medicine Hat, Alta. Ap 12, 1913, PM; 1 cent stamp, US

To: Mr. Oscar Moorman, Medicine Hat, Alberta, Canada

Hellow Nephew: How are the mumps by now. I escaped them. We have been here since Mar 27th. I like it very well. But Independence will never be like old K.N. [Knob Noster, Missouri] will it? How do you like that country? Answer. 700 South Fuller, Esther H.

Editor Note: This post card was sent to Oscar before he was married in 1918. He was 24 at this time and it's likely that he was in Canada doing brick mason work. Medicine Hat is about 1,400 miles from Independence. It's north of Great Falls, Montana.

It's unknown who Esther H. was. There is no one known as "Esther" and no one with the last name that starts with "H" on Oscar's maternal or paternal side of the family. At this time, Oscar had 13 aunts and uncles who were living who might have been the writer of this post card. It could be that the writer was asking Oscar to reply to Esther H., 700 South Fuller.

~~~

Front: A: American Falls from Below by Illumination. Niagara Falls. © Tates 23861

NIAGARA FALLS BY ILLUMINATION

Visitors now find Niagara more beautiful than ever. New radiance has been cast over it. It is a radiance that can be turned on or off at the switch of a button. As turned on each night it consists of a battery of a billion candle power which are so concealed in the foliage that they in no way mar the scenery, yet they work for hours each night flooding and lighting both the vision of the Falls and the mists above. Think what has been done to accomplish this. Power was taken from the Falls themselves and turned back upon these Falls in the form of light so that Niagara is forced to beautify itself.

Postmark: Lima, Ohio, Aug 20, 1928, 12:30 PM; 1 cent stamp

To: Mr. Oscar Moorman, 764 Undercliff Ave., Edgewater, New Jersey

Lima, Ohio, Aug. 20

We are now on our home stretch and are coming along O.K. We have had a wonderful time so far and will get home by about Wednesday. We stayed at a policeman's home in Canada. Moorman

Editor Note: This might have been from one of Oscar's siblings. The writing doesn't match Florence Geneva Moorman, his younger sister, but she was traveling in Ohio in 1928, as evidenced by a post card sent to Gela Moorman, Oscar's wife, in June 1928.

~~~

Front: 234. State Street, North from Adams Street, By Night, Chicago

This street view is midway between the current-day Willis Tower and The Art Institute of Chicago. Jackson Beach (mentioned in the post card) is south of downtown Chicago. It's on the western shore of Lake Michigan (called the old Blue Lake in the post card).

Postmark: Chicago, Ill, Aug 28, 1928, 8:30 PM; 1 cent stamp; DUE 1 CENT N.S.M.D.NO. 9*

To: Mr. Oscar Moorman, 1028 West Maple Ave., Independence, Missouri

Dear Oscar & Gela: Came up here on a little 3-day trip. We are sitting on the Beach in Jackson Park and looking over the old Blue Lake. Mother & I have been in swimming having a marvelous time. Love to Aunt Eva and all the gang. Lovingly, Lila & Mother

Editor Note: Lila is probably Oscar's cousin, Lila Blake Mount Barth Hungerford (1905-1995), and Oscar's aunt, Florence Viola Beebe Moorman Mount (1870-1953). Florence was a younger sister to Eva Estella Beebe Moorman (1868-1937), who was Oscar's mother.

*The postcard rate was increased from 1 cent to 2 cents as a wartime measure. When World War I ended at the end of 1918, the rate was lowered to its pre-War level of one cent. The postage was raised briefly from 1 cent to 2 cents in 1917-1919 and in 1925-1928; the conclusive raise to 2 cents was in 1951.

~~~

Front: Grindelwald den [Switzerland]

Postmark: 1. Canceled stamp 28 12. 2. Washington, D.C. Oct 9, 1927, 9 PM. 1. Faint and unreadable; 20 cent stamp Switzerland

To: Mr. Oscar Moorman, ~~1028 West Maple, Kansas, Independence M.o. U.S.A.~~, 764 Undercliff Ave. Edgewater, N.J.

Dear Friennd. I am left New York for Switzerland 17 Sept. [1927] and I am arrival very well in Switzerland. But I will be bag igen [back again] in Spring [April 1928] and hopp to si you agin. Your Frennd, Otto Hegi, Biel C. Switzerland

Editor Note: Herman Otto Hegi was born 29 Jul 1899 in Biel, Switzerland. He arrived in New York in April 1925 and again in April 1928. His father, Fritz, was in Biel. His siter, Lynn, was in New York. He petitioned for US citizenship in 1925 and it was granted in 1931. His occupation was listed as bricklayer. He and Oscar probably worked together.

~~~

Front: East Bridge of Venetian Way, Connecting the Beach with Belle Isle. Miami Beach, Florida

Miami Beach is located on a narrow, yet attractive peninsula. There are casinos, bathing pavilions, shore resorts and exquisite little bathing places along the ocean front, from the jetties northward, to primeval mangrove studded roads that mean "a bathing beach of your own."

The so-called Venetian Islands are a set of artificial islands located between Miami Beach and the mainland of Miami, connected by bridges, known as the Venetian Causeway. The Venetian Causeway, the arched bridge connecting the islands, is used as a popular boardwalk for exercise, jogging, hiking, pet walking, and cycling.

Postmark: Miami, Fla. Mar 2, 1929, 8:30 PM; 1 cent stamp

To: Mr. Oscar Moorman, 764 Undercliff Ave, Edgewater, N.J.

Best wishes from Mrs. Nichols, Miami, Florida, Mch [March] 1/19

Editor Note: Unknown writer.

~~~

Front: Washington Monument at Night, Washington, D.C.

The Washington Monument erected to the memory of George Washington was begun in 1848 and dedicated in 1885. It is 555 feet high, 55 feet square, and 15 feet thick at base, tapering to 34 feet square at the beginning of cap stone. Its weight is 81,120 tons. Total cost $1,275,000. The ascent may be made either by elevator or 900 steps around the sides. Memorial stones presented by several States and Territories of the U. S., foreign governments, societies, orders, and individuals are inserted in the face of the interior walls. Seen by night from across the waters of the Placid Potomac, the view is imposing and inspiring.

Postmark: Washington, D.C. 15, Jul 11, 1931, 4 PM; 1 cent stamp

To: Miss Virginia Moorman, 1028 W Maple, Independence, Mo.

July 11—Am having a interesting time hope you can see Washington some time. Daddy.

Editor Note: This post card was from Oscar Moorman to his 11-year-old daughter, Virginia. His wife, Gela, and other daughters, Enid and Eleanor, were also at the Maple address.

~~~

Front: View of St. Louis, Missouri, from the Air

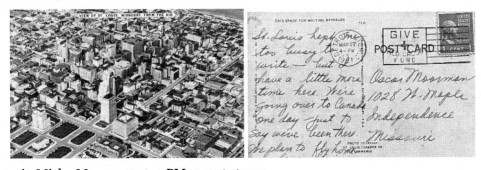

Postmark: Detroit, Mich., Mar 27, 1951, 4 PM; 1 cent stamp

To: Oscar Moorman, 1028 W. Maple, Independence, Missouri

St. Louis kept me too busy to write—but I have a little more time here. We're going over to Canada one day—just to say we've been there. We plan to fly home. Love, Ginia

Editor Note: This post card was from Virginia Moorman to her father, Oscar. She was involved with traveling nursing during this time. She also wrote a post card to her mother, Gela, at this time. The image and note are in the *Cook Family Ancestor* book.

~~~

Front: Historic Mormon Landmarks at Nauvoo, Ill.

No. 1 JOSEPH SMITH HOMESTEAD—was originally a log house, built about 1826 by James Jones, an Indian agent, who sold it to Joseph Smith in 1839. The Prophet lived there until the spring of 1843, when he moved into the Mansion House.

NO. 2. MANSION HOUSE—Built in 1842 and 1843 through revelation. Home of the Prophet at the time he was killed at Carthage, Ill., June 27, 1844. Lumber sawed near LaCrosse, Wisc., and rafted down the river.

No. 3. THE NAUVOO HOUSE—A revelation was received Jan. 17, 1841, by Joseph Smith to build it and call it the Nauvoo House. An association was incorporated Feb. 15, 1841. It was never finished. Original plan was for three stories and basement.

Postmark: Nauvoo, Ill., Aug 5, 1952; 2 cent stamp

To: Mr Oscar Moorman, 1028 W. Maple Ave, Independence, Mo

Dearest Laddie [Oscar]: Sure wish you could have stayed for the classes promise to be more wonderful all the time. We just got back from town and will mail this I bought there in the A.M. Love Gela

Editor Note: The classes that Gela referred to might have been at an RLDS church reunion or a special conference held near Nauvoo, Illinois.

~~~

Erwin Everett Moorman

Erwin Moorman

Following construction work in those days, Dad had to take us many places, and we never stayed anywhere very long before going on to the next job. While we were located at a small town, Grace Hill, Washington County, Iowa, my folks had the missionaries come and hold a three-week series. At the close of the series Oscar Ella and I were baptized along with a number of others.

[In 1920] we bought three lots just outside the city limits on Leslie Street. Our address was 825 South Leslie. There we pitched our tent and lived throughout the summer. In the fall before the winter set in we built a two room house sixteen by twenty-four feet. The floor was made of solid concrete and the walls were of four by eight by twelve clay tile . . . Later we added four more rooms and a bath. The neighbors called it the Mormon Temple.

Left: 825 South Leslie, Independence, Missouri. Right: Walnut Park RLDS Church.

When the Walnut Park [RLDS] Church was built I was given charge over the masonry work, the brick laying and the plastering. When it was all finished we had a beautiful building that would seat four-hundred people.

Mother [Hallie Moorman] had very little musical talent, but when someone gave me an old battered mandolin she learned the notes in the treble clef and how to play a few hymns. She taught me the notes too and hot to adapt them to mandolin playing. She wanted her children to be good musicians. That's how I got my start.

Oscar played the violin some, and when we played together at Religion such pieces as "The Camels Are Coming to Town" and "Turkey in the Straw" we would bring the house down. I thought we had it all made then. One day Uncle Ernest [Moorman] gave me a violin and I learned to play it quite well without any music lessons, our only text being the Hymnal and Zion's Praises [hymn book]. Now we could play along with the organ for the church services and we did this for quite a long time.

When Oscar left home and began playing cornet in a brass band I lost interest in the violin and wanted to play a cornet too. It wasn't long until Oscar bought himself a new Conn cornet and he gave his old one to me—we lived at Knobnoster then. . . .

Oscar and I found out we could play together. We played in the Knobnoster band and we worked up a number of concert duets. We did a good job of it too, if I do say so myself. We did single, double and triple tongue work with dynamics and shadings that came with natural talent combined with plenty of hard work. We did have natural musical talent and we worked hard to develop it. Dad bought us some good records and we imitated those professionals. . . .

Our whole family was musical. We all loved to sing, and many nights that house on Leslie Street rang out with hymns and other songs until late in the night. . . . Our four daughters were outstanding singers, except for Thelma who was born with a husky voice. However, they all four sang in a quartet for many years.

My sister, Ella Wood drove up from Kansas City, Kansas and brought my uncle, Ernest Moorman and my brother Oscar who laid all the masonry on the upper story [of the RLDS church we were building in Williston, North Dakota in 1958]. They were both considered among the best brick layers in Kansas City, and they put in all their time for nothing. I hope they collect on the other side. . . . We built a twenty-thousand dollar church for less than ten-thousand and it was all paid for when it was finished.

—From *Wa du ya no bout Us*

Ella Moorman Wood

Roy and Ella Wood.

Top Left—Ella and Roy. 1913.
Top Right—Ella, 1918.

Roy, Harry
Ella, at the
first Home
they Own in
K.C.K. 2940
Roosevelt.

Roy 1918.

ower Left Ella & Roy
t Camp Funston, 1918.

Roy and Ella Moorman Wood.

William Oral Moorman

We were camping about eight miles east of Osceola, Iowa when my brother Oral was born. Two nights after his birth mother had a wonderful experience. The room was filled with a choir of angles who sand a beautiful song to her, but the chorus always ended with this phrase, "Although he seemed so dear, he was only loaned for a year." The next morning mother told us that Oral would only be with us for a year. Dad tried to tell her it was only a bad dream, but mother said, No, it was all too real. It will all be fulfilled."

Just one year later, after we moved to Murray, Iowa a messenger dressed in black came to mother and told her that he had come for the boy. As mother was pleading with the messenger not to take him yet, he told her, "I will be back for him in just thirty days." The same messenger appeared to her again at the appointed time and said, "This time I will have to take him." That afternoon about two o'clock little Oral was drinking some water. He strangled and evidently burst an artery in his lungs. Three hours later he was gone. He passed very quietly from this life like one going into a quiet sleep.　　—From *Wa du ya no bout Us*

William Oral Moorman, Murray Cemetery, Iowa, died age 1.

Harry Ellsworth Moorman

Harry Moorman.

Harry and Kay Griffith Moorman.

Eva standing behind Harry and Florence Moorman.

Florence Moorman

Florence, the three year old daughter of Mr. and Mrs. E. L. Moorman, north of town, fell from a door in the barn loft, 10 or 12 feet. An ugly gash was cut on her forehead.
AUGUST 23, 1912

Jack and Florence Moorman Guy.

~~~

119

Summary of Maternal/Paternal First Generation

Oscar and Gela Moorman's Children

Virginia Merle Moorman Zukowsky Dungan

Born 7 Feb 1920 (Independence, Missouri).

David Kent Moorman born 15 Feb 1946 (Kansas City, Missouri); died 16 Feb 1975 (Destin, Florida). Cremated.

Married Anthony Joseph Zukowsky (1917; 1985) on 20 Apr 1951 (Independence, Missouri), divorced 28 Feb 1955.

Joni Merlene Zukowsky Dungan Wilson born 18 Mar 1953 (Independence, Missouri).

Susan Jane Zukowsky Dungan Barnes born 4 Sep 1954 (Independence, Missouri).

Married Alma Lafayette Dungan (1908; 1972) on 31 May 1965 (Kansas City, Missouri).

Died 15 Dec 1997 (Crestview, Florida). Cremated.

Enid Eloise Moorman Wanbaugh Cruce

Born 21 Mar 1921 (Independence, Missouri).

Married Marvin Leroy Wanbaugh (1920; 2004) on 11 Dec 1941 (Independence, Missouri); divorced.

Steven Keith Wanbaugh born 29 Jan 1946 (Independence, Missouri).

Married Louis Burnette Cruce (1926; 2000) on 14 Sep 1956 (Independence, Missouri).

Gregory Lance Cruce born 16 Oct 1957 (Independence, Missouri).

Robin Michele Rieken Golden Cruce born 24 May 1960 (Independence, Missouri).

Died 25 Feb 2003 (Independence, Missouri).

Eleanor Rose Moorman Sartwell

Born 8 Apr 1928 (Edgewater, New Jersey).

Married Bertrand Homer Sartwell (1927; 1982) on 5 Feb 1949 (Independence, Missouri), divorced.

Teresa Denise Sartwell Ewbanks Rathbun born 27 Sep 1949 (Independence, Missouri).

Dennis Charles Sartwell born 2 May 1951 (Independence, Missouri).

Laure Kay Sartwell Smith Davis born 14 May 1955 (Independence, Missouri).

Lisa Beth Sartwell Hensley born 20 Jul 1963 (Independence, Missouri).

Died 15 Jul 1987 (Independence, Missouri). Cremated.

Erwin and Ethel Moorman's Children

Helen Loduska Moorman Mengel

Born 13 Nov 1913 (Knob Noster, Missouri).

Married William Jasper Mengel (1912; 1982) on 1 Sep 1935 (RLDS Church, Independence, Missouri).

Sylvia Lynn Mengel Bryant born 1 Sep 1936 (Independence, Missouri).

Bill E. Mengel born 22 Oct 1939 (Kansas City, Missouri).

Died 4 Apr 1999 (Colorado Springs, Colorado). Buried Lee's Summit Historical Cemetery, Lee's Summit, Missouri.

Thelma Louise Moorman Kester

Born 13 Nov 1914 (Knob Noster, Missouri).

Married Forrest Henry Kester (1909; 1989) on 23 Nov 1939 (Walnut Park RLDS Church, Independence).

Geraldine Louise "Jerry Lou" Kester Martinez Sykes born 15 Aug 1941 (Missouri); died 25 Mar 1998 (Missouri).

Connie Marie Kester Zuber born 1 Oct 1945 (Kansas City, Missouri).

Died 18 Mar 2011 (Independence, Missouri). Buried Mound Grove Cemetery, Independence, Missouri.

Alta June Moorman Tousley

Born 17 Jun 1916 (Knob Noster, Missouri).

Married Kenneth Willis Tousley (1918; 1997) on 30 Jun 1939 (Walnut Park RLDS Church, Independence).

Karen Lee Tousley Hutchinson born 3 Jun 1940 (Kansas City, Missouri).

Lois Rae Tousley Brown Spurgeon born 13 Apr 1942 (Missouri); died 20 Apr 2010 (Martinsville, Indiana).

Joanna Belle Tousley Lashbrook Escalante born 20 Aug 1944 (Missouri); died 27 Aug 2018 (Texas).

Linda June Tousley Finch born 11 May 1947 (Independence, Missouri); died 8 Nov 2011 (Osceola, Iowa).

Died 6 Oct 1971 (Lamoni, Iowa). Buried Lillie Cemetery, Lamoni, Iowa.

Melba Geraldine Moorman Troyer

Born 14 Mar 1918 (Knob Noster, Missouri).

Married Albert Ronald Troyer (1919; 1998) on 4 Sep 1942 (RLDS Church, Phoenix, Arizona).

David Erwin Troyer born 6 Jan 1944 (Arkansas), adopted 22 Jul 1953; died 22 Sep 2003 (Minnesota).

Ronald Eugene "Gene" Troyer born 22 Jan 1946 (Arkansas), adopted 22 Jul 1953; died 2 Feb 2006 (Arkansas).

Died 12 Dec 2011 (Batesville, Arkansas).

Harry and Kay Moorman's Child

Sandra Kay Moorman Gates Whiteside Heeter

Born 26 Feb 1939 (Brooklyn, New York).

Married George Gates Jr. (1936; alive 2021) on 29 May (late 1950s, Lamoni, Iowa).

Married Mr. Whiteside (?-?).

Married David Heeter (1940; alive 2021) on 23 Apr 2011.

Todd Allen Gates (?-alive 2021).

Tim Gates (?-alive 2021).

Jack and Florence Guy's Children

Edward Elsworth Guy

Born 26 Aug 1934 (Santa Monica, California).

Died 21 Sep 2001 (Guatemala City, Guatemala).

Patricia Ann Guy

Born 18 Aug 1936 (Kansas City, Missouri).

Married. No children.

Eva Elizabeth Guy Greenwald

Born 15 Sep 1950 (Van Nuys, California).

Married Daniel Mark Greenwald (1950-?) on 17 Aug 1971 (Jackson County, Missouri).

Jessica Lynn Greenwald Creighton (1970s-?).

Jason C. Greenwald (1980s-?).

Made in the USA
Monee, IL
06 December 2022

19963763R00076